WAR IN BRITAIN

WAR IN BRITAIN

TIM NEWARK

ENGLISH HERITAGE

This edition specially produced
for DMG Ltd in 2002

First published by HarperCollinsPublishers 2000

HarperCollinsPublishers
77-85 Fulham Palace Road
Hammersmith
London W6 8JB

1 3 5 7 9 10 8 6 4 2

ISBN 000 765264 X

Printed and bound in Spain by Graficas Estella

CREDITS

To Victoria, always a joy to be with

The author would like to thank the following for their help with the book: Philipp Elliot-Wright, Graham Sumner, Ian Post, David Richardson, Dan Shadrake, John Harris, Kim Siddorn, Roland Williams, John Cole, Heath Pye, Mark Fry, Lynda Woodhouse, David Key, Michael Newcomen, Nigel Hardacre, Les Handscombe, Tim Rose, Geoff Carefoot, Dave Bennett, John Norris, Philip Haythornthwaite and Stephen Ede-Borrett. Thanks also to Ian Drury, the perfect editor.

Special thanks to Peter Newark.
All pictures researched by Tim Newark.

CONTENTS

INTRODUCTION

Britons love freedom and the one theme that unites all the periods of warfare in this book is their pursuit of independence. At first, it is a battle between different peoples - Celts, Saxons, Vikings - to survive within the British Isles. Then, as England takes shape as a sovereign realm, it is a struggle for political freedom between barons and kings, royalists and roundheads. Finally, with Britain as a united nation, it is the defence of its very way of life that has united its people against threats from abroad. It has been a hard and bitterly fought quest with enormous personal sacrifice by soldiers and civilians. If our island's military history has anything to tell us, it is that the freedom we have inherited must not be lightly given away.

Tim Newark

CELTS & ROMANS

From Maiden Castle in Dorset to Hadrian's Wall in Northumberland, the Celts and Romans have left their mark on Britain. Bitter battles for control of the island were followed by a long period of peace in which the two warrior peoples learned to live together.

Warfare has moulded the political and social history of Britain, and has shaped the very landscape itself, creating lines of defence, establishing historic towns astride communications routes, excavating vast amounts of earth to create hillforts and castles, leaving emblems of dominance that can be seen from the air. Some of the most enduring of these military marks on the landscape are also the most ancient.

Recreated Roman legionary of the 1st century AD stands next to a recreated late Roman soldier of the 4th century AD, showing the transformation in arms and armour. Germanic influences predominated and mail took over from segmented plate armour. They stand before a Roman wall at Richborough Castle in Kent. [Dan Shadrake /English Heritage]

The earliest recorded invaders of this country were the Celts, who arrived from France during the 7th century BC. Armed with iron weapons, some mounted on horseback, others using horses to pull light chariots, by the 1st century BC, Celtic invaders had secured their dominance over most of the land. Julius Caesar records one of the very first written accounts of life in Britain, describing a complex jigsaw of Celtic tribes in southern England, frequently fighting amongst themselves. One of the greatest untold stories is how the Celts dealt with the native Bronze Age people in Britain, and how they defeated them in battle. The clues to this very first battle for Britain are in the landscape.

Across southern England some of the most

potent signs of Celtic dominion can still be seen today. In the Vale of the White Horse in Berkshire, there is a giant white horse carved out of the chalk hillside beneath Uffington Castle, one of several such images credited to the Iron Age Celts. What did it signify?

Reconstruction of the Roman fortress of Portchester, near Portsmouth. Built around 290 BC, it was designed to defend the southern coast of Britain against Germanic pirates. [Painting by Peter Dunn/English Heritage]

Power. As when the Spanish conquistadors arrived in Mexico equipped with horses and gunpowder, the appearence of the Celts in southern England was equally dramatic; they too possessed a technological advantage over the native population.

In France and central Europe, the Celts had perfected a fast-moving form of warfare based on mastery of the horse.

Massive coastal walls of Portchester Castle defend what was known as the Saxon Shore in the 3rd century. [English Heritage]

They were superb riders and they took this one step further by inventing four-wheeled and then two-wheeled chariots. There is little evidence that the Bronze Age warriors of pre-historic Britain had experience of horses, which were native to the plains of central Europe and Asia. They probably panicked when the Celtic horsemen charged, and were cut down with long iron swords as they fled. The great white chalk horses reflect the triumph of mounted warfare. The theme is repeated in Celtic artifcacts, such as the beautifully decorated pieces of equestrian equipment that can be seen in museum collections. Even tiny Celtic coins celebrated it with galloping horses expressed as abstract dynamic lines with riders wearing cloaks flying backwards.

The other source of Celtic military power was their mastery of iron-making. Iron was developed after the use of bronze, but it produced stronger, lighter weapons with sharper blades. Iron could also be formed into rings which were then constructed into tunics of mail, a highly effective and flexible form of body armour. The Celts are usually credited with the invention of this armour in Europe, which was then adopted by the Romans. With iron swords and iron armour, the Celts possessed an enormous advantage

Aerial view of Portchester Castle demonstrating the impressive engineering of the fortress and its walls. Looking more medieval in style, it was occupied throughout the Middle Ages. The round bastions were platforms for rock and arrow-throwing artillery. [Skyscan Balloon Photography]

over Bronze Age peoples. In addition, iron enabled the manufacture of stronger tools, such as picks and spades, and this in turn allowed the Celts to build bigger and stronger hillforts with which to defend their conquests in Britain. An example of this revolution in defensive construction is evident at Maiden Castle near Dorchester.

Maiden Castle is a massive hillfort enclosing some 47 acres of a saddle-backed hill, comprising several rings of giant earth ramparts and complex gateways. It was originally developed as a small settlement by Stone Age natives on one part of the hill. The Celts took it during the 6th century BC and then set to with their iron tools, doubling the size of the settlement. They added massive ramparts constructed out of earth dug from the hillside and redistributed over wooden braced structures to create a major fortification. Several such hillforts were constructed during the period of Celtic

rule and reflect both their skills in warfare and their technical superiority.

The Celts did have one major military weakness, however. Gildas, a Celtic British chronicler of the 6th century AD, put it succinctly: 'It has always been true of this people that we are weak in beating off the weapons of the outside enemy but strong in fighting amongst each other.' Fierce tribal feuds sustained a rhythm of raid and counter-raid, creating tough soldiers but no sense of unity.
When a

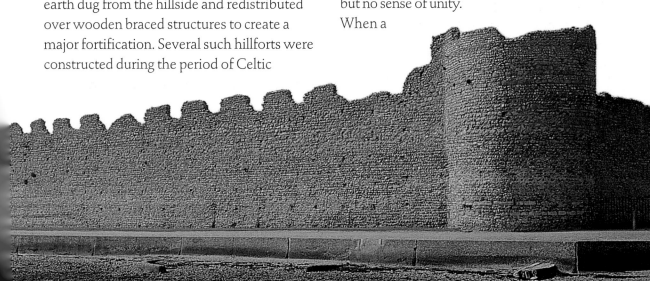

ROMAN ARMOUR

The sight of several thousand Roman soldiers all clad in armour, highly polished so that a myriad surfaces glinted in the sun, dazzling the viewer, must have sent a shiver down many a spine. Add to that the noise of several thousand pieces of armour and weapons clanging against each other as the Romans advanced, so loud that verbal commands could barely be heard, then one gets a little idea of how impressive the Roman army was in battle. And this at a time when barbarian enemies, such as the Celts or Germans, could boast only a handful of armoured warriors among them. Thus, the Romans possessed a superiority not only in the quantity and quality of arms and armour but also an unseen superiority of organisation and manufacture in which numerous armouries all over the empire could out-produce any barbarian force. It was to have a strategic effect similar to that of the Americans against the Germans in the Second World War, when the Germans

Re-enactors of the Roman Military Research Society recreate the 'tortoise', an attacking formation using shields to protect against arrows and stones as they approach an enemy fortification. Such formations were used to storm Celtic hillforts, such as Maiden Castle. [Roman Military Research Society]

might have possessed the better tanks, but the Americans could produce many more and thus overwhelmed them.

Recreating the experience of fighting in Roman armour is almost impossible, according to Graham Sumner, a member of the award-winning Ermine Street Guard re-enactment group. 'The noise is something we have recreated. Numerous legionaries marching in full armour create such a noise that we have concluded that visual and not verbal commands would have been used with musicians and standard bearers being used to convey these to ranks of soldiers virtually deafened by the sound of their own clashing arms and armour. The heat and exhaustion of moving in armour on a warm day is something we have also felt. But as for actual combat, there is so little we know. They appear to have been trained in gladiatorial forms of combat, but these seem inappropriate on the battlefield.' It is also difficult to envisage how a front rank of legionaries would be replaced by their comrades behind them, once they became exhausted, without breaking formations and causing chaos. 'Soldiers in other ranks would have thrown their spears over the swordsmen in front,' says Sumner, 'but beyond that it is difficult to guess.' Perhaps

Back of Roman legionary wearing lorica segmentata armour. This view reveals the bronze hooks, hinges and leather ties used to secure the armour plates while maintaining their flexibility. Recreations such as this demonstrate how easy it was to wear this form of armour, its weight being evenly distributed over the body, although prolonged activity on a hot day produced problems with sweat which could rot the leather ties and loosen plates. [Graham Sumner]

Reconstructed Imperial helmet of the late 1st century AD showing the magnificent horsehair crest often fitted to the helmets of more senior soldiers. [Graham Sumner]

fresher soldiers just pushed their way through the tightly packed ranks, as others fell back naturally, either wounded or tired. Certainly formations would have broken down in the scrum of hand to hand combat and become more fluid, allowing the stronger soldiers to continue the fighting as others faded.

The most famous Roman armour, seen in almost all reconstructions and visible on many remaining stone reliefs, is the lorica segmentata, strips of iron plates strapped around the arms and chest. It is a purely Roman invention and is thought, perhaps, to derive from the armour worn by gladiators in the arena, being particularly suited to protection against sword blows in close combat. Padding would have been worn under this armour to absorb the shock of a weapon's impact on the armour. Such armour was worn from the 1st to 3rd centuries AD and would have been worn throughout the conquest of Britain.

Caesar's warriors, in the first Roman expedition to Britain, wore shirts of mail, interlocking iron rings, which originated from the Celts they fought against. The difference was that Roman factories could equip every soldier with a mail shirt, whereas Celtic craftsmanship produced mail shirts only for the nobility who could afford it. Mail armour was very popular, modern reconstructions showing that a mail shirt follows the shape of the body and thus allows the wearer to take deeper breaths and wear it for longer without exhaustion than plate armour. It is also, essentially, self-cleaning, in that mail rings

Reconstructed Roman helmet of the Coolus type of the 1st century BC. Said to be inspired by Celtic helmets, it possesses both the cheekguards and neckguard incorporated in later designs. [Graham Sumner]

rub against each other, removing rust and dirt with friction. The main disadvantage of mail is that it is vulnerable to piercing weapons such as arrows; thick padding may have been worn beneath the mail to counter this.

Because the Roman army has a justifiable reputation for order and discipline, it is presumed that Roman soldiers all wore the same armour and fought with the same weapons. Recent research reveals that this was not true. Mail and plate armour were worn side by side, as many soldiers inherited or bought armour from previous generations of soldiers. Many different nationalities served in the Roman imperial army and they frequently brought their own local styles of dress and fighting with them. This might include warriors in Egypt wearing armour made out of crocodile or hippopotamus hide, or warriors from the East wearing suits of scale armour that made them look like metallic pine-cones! Then there were the measures designed by individual warriors to protect their armour or make the work of campaigning a little less uncomfortable, such as leather rags wrapped around armour and helmets, linen or woollen tubes tied on to arms, even goose feather-filled cushions worn over saddles by cavalrymen. Sweat posed one of the greatest problems on campaign as it could rust armour in a day or disintegrate leather straps so that plates just fell off. This perhaps explains why Roman soldiers preferred to fight with bare legs, thus reducing the build-up of heat beneath their body armour.

Recreated Celtic battle group. With large oval painted wooden shields held in front of them, this group of Celtic warriors is on the verge of launching a terrifying charge which they hope will break the enemy's spirit before contact is made. The Celts were renowned for this aggressive form of warfare, but if an enemy stood its ground, as the Romans did, secure in their discipline and training, then the combat would be much more difficult. [Philipp Elliot-Wright/English Heritage]

Recreated Roman legionary of the later 1st century AD. He wears the plate armour or lorica segmentata usually associated with Roman soldiers, as well as the rectangular shield. He carries both a sword and a javelin or pilum. His iron and bronze helmet is of the later Imperial type with cheekguards and a flared neckguard. The metal apron hanging from the belt is characteristic of Roman soldiers but its purpose is uncertain. It appears ornamental, although more substantial versions seem designed to protect the thighs without restricting movement. [Graham Sumner]

Vindolanda, near Hadrian's Wall, was a military base for the Roman soldiers patrolling the great northern frontier. Many everyday objects have been found there, including leather shoes bearing the stamp of their maker. [Skyscan Balloon Photography]

major new force threatened from outside, the Celts were unable to work together in alliance. This crisis had already occurred in France in the 1st century BC when Julius Caesar led his Roman armies against the Gauls. Many Gallic tribes thought they could use the Romans against their Celtic rivals and happily fought alongside Caesar until it was too late. Caesar had divided and conquered

the Celts of France and, by the 1st century AD, the Romans sought to do the same in Britain.

Caesar led a major raid on Celtic Britain in 54 BC, but it was not until AD 43 that the Romans under the Emperor Claudius undertook an invasion of Britain that would lead to its absorption into the Roman Empire. The Romans of the 1st century AD not only had the political advantage of a divided enemy, but a superior military system. The Romans were equipped with iron weapons and armour too, much of it based on Celtic models. They were certainly no better horsemen than the Celts, many of whom in fact served with them as mercenaries, but the Romans had developed a winning form of warfare based on organisation and supply. The Romans took the long view in making war. The Celts expected to win or lose in one furious combat, charging on foot or on horse with frightening shouts and yells intended to panic the enemy. The Romans withstood this form of assault through discipline and confidence in their training and weapons; having survived the initial shock, they fought back steadily and surely. Their logistic infrastructure often ensured that they had superior numbers present for the later, decisive battles of a campaign. Celtic armies could not sustain themselves in the field for the same length of time. Moving forward each day into enemy territory, establishing fortified camps and supply routes, the Romans' military professionalism brought an end to Celtic rule in Britain.

The Roman conquest of Britain began in AD 43 when 50,000 soldiers landed at Richborough in Kent under the command of Aulus Plautius. They defeated the local Celtic warlord Caractacus and crossed the Thames.

Massive earthwork walls of Maiden Castle, near Dorchester. One of the most impressive Celtic hilltop forts in Britain, it was captured by the Romans in the middle of the 1st century AD. [Skyscan]

The Emperor Claudius now joined the Roman Army, Caractacus was defeated for a second time and his capital at Colchester captured. Caractacus fled to Wales while the Romans extended their control over southern England. They measured their victories in captured hillforts, recognising these as the centres of Celtic power. The future Emperor Vespasian took command of operations westwards and the Roman historian Suetonius records that he 'subjugated two fierce tribes and captured more than twenty hillforts, including the Isle of Wight'. Maiden Castle was one of these hillforts, excavations at the eastern entrance to the site reveal the debris of battle: charred timbers and demolished earthworks. The skeletons of 38 defenders are scarred with sword and arrow cuts, the spine of one warrior being pierced by a ballista bolt.

The Romans were highly experienced in the art of siege warfare. The siege of a hillfort often began with the erection of a double line of fortifications surrounding the entire hill so as to cut off the defenders and prevent relief from outside. The Roman lines included palisades of freshly cut timber plus trenches and ramparts, a massive engineering task demanding vast amounts of labour. When the Romans considered the defenders were sufficiently weakened by hunger, they launched an attack on the weak points in the defences using artillery weapons, such as the ballista and catapult, as well as armoured Roman soldiers in their mail and iron strip armour, protecting themselves with large shields held above their heads.

By AD 49, the Romans had reached the Severn and plunged into Wales, forcing Caractacus to flee again, but a northern Celtic tribe, the Brigantes, handed Caractacus over to the Romans in return for an alliance with them against their Celtic enemies. Ten years later, the Romans destroyed the centre of the Druids on the Isle of Anglesey and marched northwards.

In AD 61 Roman rule was imperilled by a major rebellion that culminated in the sack of London and the massacre of its citizens. Boudicca, or Boadicea as she has been called in later history, was the widow of the Celtic king of the Iceni who ruled East Anglia. Roman tax-collectors ransacked the dead king's realm and had Boudicca whipped when she protested; her daughters were raped. With the support of her own and other outraged Celtic tribesmen, Boudicca led a revolt against the Romans, taking advantage of the fact that Paullinus, the Roman Governor, had moved most of his troops to north Wales.

Roman Colchester was the first target of Boudicca's fury and after a two day battle the settlement was annihilated and its inhabitants slaughtered. Paullinus moved south as fast as he could, but it was too late for the Roman inhabitants of London and St Albans who

Roman bath at Bath. The Romans were bewitched by the natural heated spring waters that bubbled up from the ground near the river Avon and built a massive bathing and religious complex around it. [English Heritage]

were put to the sword by Boudicca's tribesmen. Paullinus finally confronted Boudicca near Lichfield. The Celts, typically, began the battle with a wild, howling charge, Boudicca mounted on a war chariot. The Roman historian Dio Cassius describes Boudicca as 'very tall, most terrifying in appearance, a fierce eye and harsh voice. A great mass of the tawniest hair fell to her hips. Around her neck she wore a golden torc and over a multi-coloured tunic she wore a thick cloak secured with a brooch'. The Romans withstood the assault, flinging javelins at the Celts, then closing with their short stabbing swords. It was a battle of no clever manoeuvres, just sheer hard fighting, and the professional Roman soldiers prevailed. Boudicca, her army disintegrating before her, could see no way out and, according to the Roman historian Tacitus, committed suicide by taking poison.

Boudicca's revolt was the last great act of resistance by the British Celts towards the Roman conquest, but the defeat of the Celts was not a calamity for all Celtic people. Roman rule provided a degree of peace and stability that had been missing in the years of tribal conflict and this triggered a growth in prosperity. Meanwhile, so long as the Celtic chieftains paid their taxes to the Romans, they were allowed to continue in their positions of local power.

The Roman conquest of Britain came to a halt in the 2nd century AD. The Romans now ruled an empire that stretched from Wales to Syria and their thoughts turned to the preservation of the way of life they had established,

Close-up of the famous leather boots worn by the ordinary Roman legionary as he marched across Europe. Typical of the style worn in the 1st century AD, they feature hobnails on the soles to protect the leather. Three layers of tanned ox or cow hide were used to construct such boots, the tanning process itself taking two years. Egyptian records state that pairs of boots were issued three times a year to each soldier. [Graham Sumner]

A column of Roman soldiers advances through the British countryside. The presence of armoured, organised formations of Roman soldiers must have been an awesome sight for the native British, used to a more casual form of raiding warfare. These re-enactors belong to the Ermine Street Guard, the oldest and most highly respected of British living history groups recreating the life of Roman soldiers in Britain. [Philipp Elliot-Wright/ English Heritage]

rather than seeking new territory. Such concerns were in the mind of the Emperor Hadrian when he visited northern Britain in AD 122. A large timber building with fifty rooms, some decorated with painted walls, was erected for his stay (the remains of this have recently been uncovered at the Vindolanda site at Chesterholm) and the Augustan History captures the bold idea that caught his imagination: 'Having reformed the army of the Rhine in regal manner, he set out for Britain where he put many things to rights and was the first to build a wall, eighty miles in length, by which barbarians and Romans should be divided.' It has been suggested that the idea might even have come to Hadrian, who was a lover of the exotic, when he heard about the Great Wall in China. Certainly, there are architectural similarities between the two.

Work began on Hadrian's Wall almost immediately, starting from a bridge over the river Tyne at Newcastle and stretching right across northern Britain to the village of

Roman tent and equipment of the late 1st century AD. Such tents were made of leather sections that were stitched so the seams overlapped and were thus waterproof. Each soldier carried a wooden stake which could be tied together with others, like those on the extreme left of the picture, to form sharp barriers which could be erected around the encampment every night. These re-enactors belong to the recreated Legio II Augusta. [Legio II Augusta]

Bowness on the Solway Firth. The first section, as far as the river Irthing, just over forty miles, was built of stone, but then the materials ran out and the rest of the thirty miles was completed with earth ramparts. Later, however, this was replaced with a stone wall. Ditches were dug on the northern side to add to the obstacle. At every Roman mile (1,481 metres), a little stone fort was built to house the garrisons of from eight to 64 soldiers that had to guard that section of the wall. Two look-out turrets were added at regular intervals in the space between the fortlets. As well as adding a further four miles of wall from Newcastle to Wallsend on the east coast, 16 major forts were built behind the frontier line, the largest being at Stanwix, near Carlisle, which could maintain some 9,000 men.

Although an impressive work of military engineering that has survived in substantial sections over 2,000 years, the purpose of Hadrian's Wall was less about preventing barbarians from entering Roman Britain than about regulating their access. In reality, it

ROMAN WEAPONS

The most famous Roman weapon is the gladius, a short straight double-edged blade with a long point, effective for both stabbing and slashing. Roman chroniclers declared that this style of weapon was derived from the Celts, but it has since become identified with the Roman soldier who used it in combination with his large rectangular shield (another Celtic influence). The average blade length of these swords was about 500 mm. Roman cavalrymen used a longer, slashing sword called the spatha. A purely Roman invention was the pilum, a throwing spear with a narrow iron neck attached to its wooden shaft. The thin iron neck would bend on impact, thus denying the enemy the chance of throwing

the spear back and also, ideally, weighing down his shield, so he could not fight effectively with it and would have to throw it down. Archery did not come naturally to the Romans and so they employed archers from their conquered territories, particularly

Close-up of reconstruction of a beautifully decorated scabbard of a Roman sword based on an example found in the River Thames at Fulham. [Graham Sumner]

Reconstructed Roman mobile artillery piece. Such a weapon worked like a crossbow and launched a large bolt at the enemy. The crew are members of the Roman Military Research Society who recreate soldiers of Legio XIIII Gemina, one of the four legions originally involved in the invasion of Britain in AD 43, who also fought against Boudicca in the most dangerous Celtic revolt of the period. [Roman Military Research Society]

from the East where there was a strong tradition of archery. The most widely used bow was a composite bow in which the wooden structure was strengthened by strips of sinew and bone, giving it greater elasticity and tension. Recent tests have shown how effective arrows were against armour, penetrating both mail and scale armour, but not iron plate. Surprisingly, wooden shields with a leather covering also proved highly effective, preventing a lethal penetration. A

Excellent example of a reconstructed suit of Roman scale armour made out of hundreds of little bronze overlapping scales sewn onto a fabric tunic. This particular suit with a hood is inspired by a 3rd century AD fresco in the Middle East and is an indication of later styles of armour worn in Roman Britain. [Graham Sumner]

Roman soldier equipped with both lorica segmentata and a shield could be almost impervious to enemy archery.

Field artillery appears to have been a Roman speciality. Whereas catapults and ballistae had been used by many armies at sieges, the Romans made lighter versions of these stone- and arrow-throwing weapons and placed them in front of their troops to let off frightening volleys before the main combat, just as European armies would use cannons centuries later. Modern reconstructions have shown how effective these weapons could be, hurling heavy bolts over long distances so that even if they did not impale an enemy they would skid and bounce on the ground, causing mayhem in enemy lines.

would have been impossible to defend the wall with the same intensity of force as a castle - a few soldiers in the middle of nowhere could do little to stop a determined breach of the wall - but the physical barrier meant that anyone who wished to cross the border had to pass through guarded gateways. Traders could be taxed on their goods.

The rest of Roman Britain was controlled by a network of forts, each housing a legion or smaller Roman force. Typical of these was the Roman fort at Caerleon in south Wales near Newport. It was founded under the Emperor Vespasian whose legion, II Augusta, had played such an important part in capturing the Celtic hillforts of southern England. He wished to see the conquest of the Silures in Wales and ordered his general Sextus Julius Frontinus to execute the campaign. Frontinus needed a base near the Welsh coast so ships could bring supplies and men to his army and he chose a site on the river Usk. Initially, the rectangular fortress that was built around AD 75 was constructed of timber and earth ramparts with a wooden palisade above it, not too dissimilar to a Celtic hillfort,

but as the campaign in Wales succeeded, a more long-term construction of stone walls with towers was built. It became the home of II Augusta whose over 5,000 soldiers occupied a complex including barracks, workshops, granaries, a hospital and baths. For entertainment, an amphitheatre was constructed outside the walls where the soldiers and locals could enjoy gladiatorial combats and other less bloody shows. Remains of the barracks, baths and walls can still be seen today, along with the amphitheatre, which in the Middle Ages gained the reputation of being the original Round Table of Arthur and his knights.

Roman rule in Britain continued until the 4th century AD. For many Celtic and Roman landlords, life in Britain was better than it was in mainland Europe where, from France to the Balkans, invasions by German and Turkic tribes were becoming depressingy frequent. Britain was insulated from this chaos and a strong Romano-British army was able to counter attacks by barbarian raiders. German pirates posed a threat, but a series of castles was erected along the southern and eastern coast of England, creating a line of defence known as the Litus Saxonicum or Saxon Shore. The best preserved of these fortresses are at Pevensey and Portchester; their massive stone walls and tall towers look more like medieval castles. The Roman fort at Portchester near Portsmouth is almost a perfect rectangle with rounded bastions built into the walls

Section of Hadrian's Wall near Cawfields. Although impressive in scale and construction, it was never intended purely as a military defence, but more as a way of regulating trade between north and south.
[Skyscan/English Heritage]

Celtic warriors jeer and taunt their enemy. Insults hurled before a battle were an important way of testing an oppo-
nent's morale and also strengthening one's own courage. The recreated warrior on the left wears a shirt of mail plus a
bronze helmet, while the warrior in the middle goes into battle stripped to the waist. Tattoos and body painting were
popular among Celtic warriors. [Philipp Elliot-Wright/English Heritage]

which could mount bolt-throwing artillery to harass pirates.

Towards the end of the 4th century, barbarian tribes such as the Picts, Scots and Saxons began to act in alliance, or at least seem to have coordinated their attacks, menacing several parts of Roman Britain at the same time and stretching the defence forces to breaking point. In AD 410, Roman rule officially came to an end with a letter from the Emperor Honorius telling the Romano-Britains to look after themselves; Rome could no longer defend them as the great city itself had been sacked by the Visigoths. It was a blow to Roman administration in Britain, but there were too many local landlords who enjoyed the Roman style of life for it to change overnight. The change came slowly as Saxon raiders became settlers and a Germanic influence grew stronger among the ruling families.

SAXONS AND VIKINGS

With the end of Roman rule in Britain, a number of Germanic and Scandinavian invaders fought for control of the island, including Saxons, Angles and Vikings. Their period of rule is often called the Dark Ages, but their literature and craftwork reveals tales of great heroes.

Saxons, Jutes, Angles, and Frisians, all from tribes in what is now the Netherlands or Denmark, crossed to late Roman Britain in increasing numbers. Some came for plunder, others to serve the Romano-British as mercenaries. It has been claimed that the Saxon conquest of Britain in the 5th century brought in a new era of 'Britishness', that the Romano-Celtic people were superseded by a Germanic nation, thus giving birth to the 'Anglo-Saxon' people.

If King Arthur existed in the late 5th century AD, which seems likely, then this is what his warriors would have looked like. Essentially late Roman in style, they have elements of arms and armour influenced by Germanic warriors at the time such as the Saxons.
[Dan Shadrake]

This was developed by some 19th century historians who favoured the idea of a Germanic base to British culture rather than a Celtic or Mediterranean one, perhaps because the British royal family happened to be of German origin. Such a vision is untrue.

The Saxon conquest of Britain in the 5th century took the form of a mercenary revolt in which a handful of Germanic warlords, Hengist being the most prominent, seized the estates of their Romano-British paymasters. Recent genetic research reveals that the majority of modern British people are of Celtic, not Germanic origin. The Saxon conquest of Britain was a struggle between a Saxon elite and a Romano-British elite. Nevertheless, the Saxon conquest was a war

Armoured Saxon warrior of the 10th century. His sun wheel shield design is based on those seen in contemporary Saxon manuscripts. [Regia Anglorum]

in which the most famous character of early British history figured prominently: Arthur. Despite the recent discovery of an ancient piece of slate bearing the name 'Artognou', all we really know about the King Arthur of legend is a list of twelve battles he fought throughout Britain. All the classic tales about Merlin, Guinevere, and Lancelot were composed by later medieval authors such as Sir Thomas Malory who wrote Le Morte D'Arthur in the 15th century. Around AD 460, there is record of a Romano-British warlord called Ambrosius Aurelianus who commanded a force of noble horsemen protecting their West Country and Welsh estates from Saxon raiders. Arthur was probably of a similar background and took over from Ambrosius when he died. Arthur was a Christian, described by the chronicler Nennius, as carrying 'the image of the holy Mary, the Everlasting Virgin, on his shield'.

The climax of Arthur's campaign against the Saxons was the battle of Badon Hill. Nennius describes the hot water that bubbled up at the natural springs of Badon as one of the wonders of Britain and it is possible that this was the Roman settlement of Bath. The battle lasted three days and may well have been a siege of the town by Saxons. Arthur broke the stalemate by leading a cavalry charge against the Saxons, slaughtering many of them and stopping Saxon raids on the West Country for at least two decades.

The conversion of the Anglo-Saxons to Christianity in the late 6th century did not bring an end to the conflict, but fuelled a new one with the Saxons intent on crushing the Celtic church. At the battle of Chester, an army of Northumbrian Anglo-Saxons massacred 1,200 Celtic monks from a monastery in Bangor. 'Though they carry no arms,' said the Saxon warlord, trying to justify the atrocity, 'those monks by crying to their God still fight against us.' Celtic pirates from Ireland called Scotti added to the chaos, assaulting both Saxons and Britons on the west coast from Wales to Scotland. In western Scotland, these Irish raiders established settlements and eventually displaced the native Picts, giving

their name to the land.

The original name of the Irish settlement in north western Scotland was Dalriada, centred on the hillfort of Dunadd, sited on a rocky outcrop surrounded by boggy land. The Scots and Picts fought each other for hundreds of years. Based on the evidence of inscribed stone monuments, especially that in the churchyard of Aberlemno, the Picts fought in a distinct manner. They favoured both square and round shields, the square shields being decorated with swirling Celtic patterns, and when faced by cavalry, they formed into a kind of phalanx in which men armed with long spears or pikes protected warriors in the front line armed with shields and swords. The use of long spears carried by soldiers in dense formations became a characteristic of Scots warfare and reoccurred in the later Middle Ages, when the formation was known as a schiltron.

The Picts defended their land with tall stone chimney-like fortifications called brochs. These had no windows, only a door, but were perfect for herding one's livestock and family into at a moments notice when Scots raiders were sighted. The Picts were not always on the defensive and in 740, the Annals of Ulster record a major assault on Dalriada when the Pictish warlord Angus mac Fergus captured the stronghold and drowned the Scots commander, forcing others to row back to northern Ireland. Eventually, the close contact between the Picts and Scots blurred relations and periods of peace saw intermarriage between the aristocratic families of both sides. In 843 the Scots king Kenneth mac Alpin succeeded to the throne of the Picts. Elsewhere in Britain, the line between Celt and Saxon was still

POETIC WARRIORS

English poems and Celtic myth cycles provide a remarkably intimate view of what it was like to be a warrior. Take for example The Wanderer, an anonymous Anglo-Saxon poem, which opens with the image of a man sailing alone, across a winter sea.

'As I recall the slaughter of my comrades, there is no one I can open my heart to. The man mindful of his reputation does not reveal his sadness. Ever since I buried my lord, ever since I lost my companions, I must mourn alone. Now I have left my home land, I sail the icy seas in search of a new lord. A generous giver of gold. A lord who will welcome me into his drinking-hall and divert me from grief.'

He lists the virtues a good, mature warrior should possess, but above all, he must accept the passing of time. 'Wealth is fleeting, comrades are fleeting. Man is transient.' It is an enormously melancholic poem and one can imagine that it was written to be recited to older warriors, seated around a table crowded with drinking cups, express-

Viking boat recreated by re-enactment group Regia Anglorum. The Vikings were excellent sailors and graduated from simply coastal boats to magnificent ocean-going ships that could sail all the way to North America. [Regia Anglorum]

ing their own feelings of sadness at the end of their youth and the onset of uncertain middle age.

The spectacle of warfare is captured vividly in the 8th century epic Beowulf, the longest surviving poem written in Old English. The hero is a Geat, an inhabitant of either Denmark or Sweden, and he battles against a monster called Grendel, but the context is one of raids and counter-raids, the very stuff of early medieval combat. The Geats arrive by boat: 'Boar-heads glittered on glistening helmets Above their cheek-guards, gleaming with gold.' Animal ornaments were believed to confer special powers on their wearers and the helmets described are typical of types found at Coppergate in York and at Sutton Hoo, known as a Ridge-type helmet based on Late Roman models. The Geats are welcomed by a friendly warlord, giving the poet ample opportunity to describe their equipment: 'Bright were their byrnies, hard and hand-linked; In their shining armour the chain-mail sang... The sea-weary sailors set down their shields, Their wide, bright bucklers along the wall... Their stout spears stood in a stack together Shod with iron and shaped of ash.' A byrny was a shirt or tunic of mail, the poet drawing attention to the hand-linked rings that made it up, and this was the principal form of armour worn at this time by professional warriors. They also carried broad, wide round shields with a protruding metal boss in the middle which could be used as an offensive weapon in the crush of hand-to-hand combat. Spears were the most common of

Recreated battle group of Picts with wardogs. Dominating most of Scotland until the arrival of the Irish Scots, they fought many successful campaigns against the Angles of northern England. [Dan Shadrake/English Heritage]

weapons, swords being more costly and the sign of higher status.

Beowulf triumphs over his monstrous enemies, but eventually he too faces death and is given a warlord's burial. His followers 'fashioned a mound Broad and high on the brow of the cliff, Seen from afar by sea-faring men. Ten days they worked on the warrior's barrow Inclosing the ash of the funeral flame... They bore to the barrow the rings and the gems, The wealth of the hoard the heroes had plundered' [Translation of Beowulf is by Charles W. Kennedy, first published 1940]. Over a thousand years later, just such a funeral barrow was excavated at Sutton Hoo near Woodbridge in Suffolk and inside was found the helmet, armour, weapons and gems of a 7th century Saxon warrior. This, the most famous archaeological discovery of this period, now lies in the British Museum and provides solid visual evidence for what a warlord such as Beowulf would have looked like.

strong and in the 8th century Offa, Saxon king of Mercia, gave physical reality to the cultural divide by erecting a massive earth rampart that ran the length of the Welsh border from Treuddyn to Chepstow. It was not a fortified barrier like Hadrian's Wall but served more as a boundary marker discouraging cattle raiders. Today, it is called Offa's Dyke.

Either side of Offa's Dyke, Northern Wales was dominated by the principality of Gwynedd, with Powys lying to the northeast next to Mercia. In the south of Wales, Dyfed covered Pembroke and the west coast, while Gwent included the south-east. Cornwall remained an independent Celtic realm. In Saxon England, the two dominant powers were Mercia in the midlands and Wessex in the south. The original Germanic settlements of Sussex (south Saxons), Essex (east Saxons), and East Anglia (east Angles) lay on the east coast, while the north of England was under the control of Northumbria. The Saxons had won the better land from the Celts, commanding the great lowland areas of rich agriculture and the major trading centres and this, in the long run, would see the Saxon kings become stronger and richer, while the Celts never possessed the resources to challenge them. Both Celts and Saxons, however, were challenged by a new force which entered Britain in the 8th century AD: the Vikings.

In 793, the Laud Chronicle, one of the famous Anglo-Saxon chronicles, records strange events.

'In this year, terrible portents appeared over Northumbria and miserably frightened the inhabitants. There were flashes of lightning and fire-breathing dragons were seen flying in the air. A great famine followed these signs and a little after that raiding heathens destroyed God's church in Lindisfarne by rapine and slaughter.'

The Vikings had arrived. According to later historians, this was the beginning of the Viking age in Britain, but what is puzzling is why the arrival of these Scandinavian raiders should be considered different from the Danish and Germanic raiders who had appeared before?

Array of recreated weapons of the Dark Ages period in Britain. From left to right: Saxon seax with bone handle; seax with copper alloy fittings; Pictish sword; two Roman spatha-style swords; broad-headed spear.
[Derek Clow]

The first answer, of course, is that they were not; they were just given a different name by later historians. But from the point of view of their contemporaries, these later Scandinavian warriors were different in one important respect: they were pagans. Saxon and Celtic Britain was Christian. The Vikings came at first as raiders, seizing treasure and slaves. Their ships would land on a beach and with horses, either brought with them or stolen, they would ride into the hinterland until they had gathered more goods than they could carry. Why the Viking raids expanded into wholesale wars of conquest is still the subject of intense historical debate. The political cohesion of many kingdoms was eroded by years of Viking attacks, the Vikings enjoyed certain strategic and tactical advantages, and there were probably events within Scandinavia that helped precipitate a dramatic change in the scale of Viking incursions. The Laud Chronicle recorded in alarm,

'And the heathen stayed in Thanet over the winter. And the same year [851] came 350 ships to the mouth of the Thames, and stormed Canterbury, and put to flight Beorhtwulf, king of Mercia, with his levies, and went then south over the Thames into Surrey.'

Aethelwulf of Wessex eventually defeated this force, but by the second half of the 9th century, Viking warlords had conquered the land around York, laid claim to half of Mercia, and held all of East Anglia.

In Wessex, the last Saxon realm to resist the Vikings, King Alfred led a determined defence, but even he was overwhelmed and forced to flee to the shelter of the marshes in Somerset. He organised guerrilla resistance, but it was through diplomacy as well as military skill that he eventually triumphed. He penned the Vikings into a fort at Chippenham, where they awaited a crushing blow, but instead Alfred invited the leading Vikings to his camp. There, he declared that if the Vikings accepted the Christian faith and left Wessex, he would spare their lives and let them live in the eastern part of England. The Vikings accepted the offer and their realm became known as the Danelaw. Alfred even-

Recreated Viking raiding party comes inland on the marshy flats outside Wareham. They are well equipped with helmets, mail, swords and spears and are typical of warriors of the 10th century. [Regia Anglorum]

RECREATING ARTHUR'S KNIGHTS

When it comes to portraying King Arthur and the Knights of the Round Table at the cinema or on television, he is usually shown wearing a shining suit of plate armour. This portrayal is true of when Thomas Malory wrote Le Morte D'Arthur as this kind of beautiful armour was typical of the 15th century. But the original Arthur, on which all the later legends and tales have been based, was a warlord living towards the end of the 5th century. What would he and his warriors really have looked like?

Dan Shadrake of Britannia, the leading re-enactment group of this early medieval period, has devoted much time and effort to gathering the evidence and then using it to

recreate the authentic arms and armour of the Arthurian period. The result is a figure that looks more Roman than a medieval knight. 'The main influence which preceded the Britain of Arthur was that of Rome,' states Shadrake. 'The later Roman Empire provides the material with which Arthurian Britain can be tentatively reconstructed.'

The main forms of body armour were mail or tunics made out of scale or lamellar armour, both of Eastern origin. A kilt of leather strips would then have hung from the waist protecting the upper thighs, just like that worn by Roman legionaries in earlier centuries. Iron helmets with a nasal and cheekguards would have been of the Sassanian or Ridge type or the more Germanic spangenhelm segmented form. Germanic influence was strong in the form of spatha-style, long double-edged swords. Shields were large and oval, made of wood reinforced with iron and probably adorned with Christian emblems such as the crucifix or the Madonna.

Reconstructed spangenhelm with nasal of the type worn by both Vikings and Normans. It was an enormously popular form of helmet that continued to be worn as late as the 13th century. Recreated by Russell Thomas and Chris Lydamore. [Dan Shadrake]

Norman knights charge at the recreated Battle of Hastings. Although the warriors here carry their lances underarm in later medieval fashion, many lances would have been thrown overarm during the battle, the word lance deriving from the French verb to throw. [Alan Jeffrey]

tually united Saxon England by having his daughter marry the ruler of Mercia. For this reason, Alfred was later dubbed 'the Great' by British historians, the only English monarch to receive that honour. The high point of Saxon rule was reached under Alfred's son, Edward, who by 918 had won back all the Danish settlements and united England under one king.

A flavour of the fighting between Saxon and Viking is conveyed by the 10th century poem The Battle of Maldon. Fought in 991, the battle took place in Essex in south-east England. The Vikings under the command of Svein Forkbeard, king of Denmark, had sailed with an army of some 4,000 warriors in 93 ships and entered the Blackwater Estuary near the town of Maldon. They camped on Northey Island and expected to cross the

causeway to ravage the hinterland. Before them stood Byrhtnoth, the local Saxon war-lord, and his hastily assembled force. In order to fight a defensive battle, Byrhtnoth ordered his leading warriors to dismount and form a shield wall in which the warriors stood close to each other so their large round shields overlapped each other. Byrhtnoth was a white-haired man of about sixty and a land-lord of considerable wealth, but this did not prevent him from taking his place among younger warriors in the shield wall.

The confrontation with the Vikings began with an exchange of insults. This may well

be a poetic device to raise the tension for an audience, but it may also be true of ancient warfare in which warriors would jeer and rush forward out of their line to show their lack of respect for the opposition. The Vikings declared they would be happy to leave if the Saxons gave them a tribute of gold. 'Listen pirates,' replied Byrhtnoth, 'the only tribute we shall send you is one of spear-points and veteran sword-edge. We are the guardians of our people, our land and our King. It is the heathen who shall fall.' Arrows followed the insults, but the Vikings had a problem. They could not leave the island to cross the narrow causeway while the Saxons defended it. They asked permission to cross the water and begin the battle on a more equal footing. Amazingly, and over-confidently, according to the poet, Byrhtnoth allowed the enemy to cross over onto the mainland. This decision may not have been so crazy as it seems, for, denied combat here, the Vikings could easily have sailed elsewhere, whereas at least the Saxons were ready for them now.

Dubbed Wolves of Wodan, the Norse God of War, by the poet, the Vikings wade across the ford with their lime-wood shields and

weapons held high. The battle begins with the loosing of arrows and flinging of spears. Immediately, the Saxon leader Byrhtnoth comes under attack. A 'southern spear', meaning a spear made in France, wounds the Saxon lord but he breaks the shaft with the edge of his shield and throws his own spear which plunges into the Viking attacker's neck. Byrhtnoth bellows with laughter and thanks God for his good luck, but is then attacked again and wounded for a second time with a thrown spear. A comrade pulls out the spear and throws it back at the Dane. Yet another Viking closes in, determined to steal the rich mail armour and sword from the wounded lord, but Byrhtnoth swings his sword at the assailant. The Dane parries the blow and slashes at the Saxon's arm, so that he drops his gold-hilted sword and, under

more blows, Byrhtnoth and his closest warriors are killed.

Seeing the death of their lord, many of the Saxons lose their nerve and one, disgracefully, even steals the horse of his dead chief to escape. The poet notes that Byrhtnoth had generously given this man many horses in the past. Many warriors remain, however, and the fighting grows fiercer. A noble hostage from a Northumberland family proves his worth by wounding the Vikings with his bow and arrows. Mail shirts ring and split under sword blows, shields shatter leaving warriors to punch their enemies with the

Pictish crossbowman recreation based on the figure on the Drosten stone of the 8th or 9th centuries AD. Although associated with later periods, there is evidence that crossbows were used by the Romans. It is a simple crossbow with a rising peg trigger and wooden prod. [Lyn Smith]

Saxon archer hunting with long wooden bow. At his side he wears a long single-edged sword or seax, typical of Saxon warriors. Archery was used in battle to harass the enemy and provoke them into combat. [Regia Anglorum]

remaining metal bosses. With their lord gone, the Saxons are doomed, but it is an heroic last stand and a veteran warrior expresses the virtues expected of a loyal fighting man:

'Heart must be braver, courage the bolder, mind the firmer, as our strength becomes lesser. Here lies our lord. A noble man, in blood and mud. Those who turn their back now will regret it forever. I am old. I will not leave here. I will lie beside my lord — the man I love most dearly.'

Having battled the Vikings valiantly and with considerable success for some two hundred years, the Saxons finally succumbed to a Danish King in 1013. His son, Canute, ruled a Scandinavian empire that included England, the Scottish islands, Greenland, Norway and Denmark.

Elsewhere in northern Europe, another dynasty of Vikings had done very well for themselves. These were the Northmen of northern France or Normans. In the 9th century, they advanced deep into France, attacked Paris, and the French monarchy eventually made a deal with them. The Northmen recognised French rule, but received land of their own in what became known as Normandy. The fate of this realm and England soon became intertwined. A son

of the last Saxon king of England, Edward, was brought up in the Norman court and became king of England in 1042. Edward, however, left the rule of his country largely to a powerful noble family called Godwin and principally Harold, who harboured royal ambitions. When Edward died, Harold assumed the throne. William duke of Normandy, claimed that both Edward and Harold had promised it to him. The stage was set for the most famous invasion in British history.

Crowned in January 1066, Harold was soon under attack from different directions. William assembled an invasion force in Normandy. Harold's estranged brother Tostig

MAKING MAIL

Mail, or 'chain-mail' as it has been wrongly called, was the main form of armour worn throughout the early medieval period in Britain. Saxons, Vikings and Normans all wore mail tunics, sometimes longer, sometimes shorter, but all essentially made of interlinking iron rings. The process of making mail was time-consuming and required some skill, thus making mail shirts expensive and well worth looting from dead warriors on a battlefield.

Making mail began with the construction of the rings, which was achieved by winding iron wire tightly around a metal bar. This coil was then chopped off the bar to produce open-ended links. The links were forced through a tapering hole until they overlapped. The ends of the overlap were hammered flat with a small chip of metal inserted in a hole in the overlap to form a rivet. The closed rings were then linked with open-ended links which were then similarly hammered together. Each ring was linked with four others and thus a dense flexible armour was built up in the T-shape of a shirt. Fringes of brass or even gilded rings, some with lucky or magical words inscribed on them, were added to the most expensive forms of mail shirt.

Recreated late Roman officer c. AD 400. He wears lamellar armour made out of numerous little plates laced together. His helmet is of the Sassanian or Heavy Ridge type with a nasal and broad cheek-guards. [Dan Shadrake/English Heritage]

Making mail armour in the traditional way. Mail was the most popular armour in the early medieval period in Britain and consisted of numerous inter-linked rings. It was a complex and costly process to make a mail shirt and only the wealthier warriors wore such armour. [Regia Anglorum]

raided the south coast of England before sailing to Norway. There he allied himself with the king, Harold Hardrada who planned an invasion of his own. All summer Harold kept his army and fleet on the alert. The Norwegians landed first, together with their English allies, capturing York in early September. Harold rushed northwards and caught them off guard at Stamford Bridge. Both Tostig and the king of Norway were slain in the rout. Harold's triumph was short-lived, however; three days later, the duke of Normandy landed at Pevensey on the East Sussex coast.

Harold marched south at impressive speed to arrive with some 6,000 men about 12 miles inland from Pevensey. A present-day war journalist with experience of marching with peasant armies in Afghanistan has recently contended that, like the mujahideen, medieval footsoldiers were used to exertions that would exhaust modern men and the English probably arrived fit for battle. In any case, many of them were mounted. Whether Harold was hoping to make another surprise attack will never be known. His arrival detected the previous afternoon, on the morning of October 14th, Harold assembled his army in a defensive formation: a shield wall on the crest of Senlac Hill.

The battlefield of Hastings is well pre-served today and it needs little imagination to see how the hillside must have handicapped the Norman attack. William began the combat with a storm of arrows and then sent his armoured cavalry forward to test the shield wall, flinging their lances as spears, but the English remained unmoved. The steep slope weakened the impact of the Norman charge and by the end of the morning William was

Recreation of Viking settlement. Once Viking raids on Britain proved successful, many Vikings decided to settle on land conquered in the eastern part of the country. [The Vikings (N.F.P.S.)]

in trouble. Under the hail of arrows, stones, and spears, it was rumoured that the duke had been killed and he was forced to lift his helmet and ride before his men to prove he lived. Warfare often hinges on psychological moments when fear overwhelms confidence and this was particularly so in medieval battles when kings and commanders fought in the lines with their troops. Bretons in the service of the Duke had broken and were pursued by English sensing victory, but the counter-attack was poorly judged and

William cut them down with his cavalry.

William ordered his troops up the hill again and again. Finally, Harold's shield wall faltered and Normans broke in among his warriors. Furious hand-to-hand combat ensued, axes and swords clashed, arm muscles burned and weakened. Harold was himself wounded by an arrow in his right eye, but his personal bodyguard of housecarls stoutly defended him, armed with long two-handed Viking-style battleaxes and shouting 'Out! Out! Out!' A group of

Norman knights now saw the opportunity for great honour and concentrated on breaking through to Harold. In the turmoil, Harold's royal banner fell to the ground and four Norman knights finally pushed into the tight circle around him, hacking at the wounded Harold until his body was dismembered. The spirit of the English was broken and though many fought on, the battle came to an end as the English line disintegrated and Normans hunted the fleeing soldiers mercilessly through the night.

Recent evidence shows that Hastings was not the only battle William had to fight before he was crowned king of England. Archaeological discoveries in the City of London have revealed the bodies of English soldiers killed in a battle fought on land beneath the north side of St. Paul's Cathedral. Such was London's resistance to the Normans that

one chronicler records that William was forced to construct siege towers and battering rams. English traitors eventually opened the gates of the city to William, but a considerable body of soldiers resisted his advance. The Normans triumphed, but it had been hard work and one can speculate that if the English had survived a siege successfully, an English warlord may well have cut off William and reversed the decision achieved at Hastings. However, on Christmas Day 1066, William was crowned king of England in Westminster Abbey. A Norman dynasty now ruled Britain.

Recreated Norman crossbowmen are paid for their services by a Norman knight. Mercenaries were always an important element of medieval armies, helping to swell the numbers recruited through feudal vows of service.
[Hannah Jenkins]

The battle of Hastings recreated on the actual battle-field in Sussex. In this scene, English warriors have charged down from the shield wall on the ridge of the hill to attack the faltering Bretons, but the Normans launch a counter-attack which severely shakes English resolve. [Peter Newark's Military Pictures]

Viking shield wall. The supreme defensive formation of the Dark Ages, it was a shield wall such as this that Harold deployed at Hastings and resisted several attacks by the Normans. [Regia Anglorum]

Saxon and Viking clash during a Viking raid, recreated by members of Regia Anglorum. Both sides wore similar arms and armour, including short mail shirts and large round shields. [Regia Anglorum]

TESTING MEDIEVAL WARFARE

The recreation of early medieval arms and armour by numerous re-enactment groups has allowed the testing of medieval combat tactics. Dan Shadrake of Britannia has found the experience illuminating, confirming several truths of medieval warfare but also shattering a few illusions. 'What was no surprise to us,' says Shadrake, 'was that armoured footsoldiers in disciplined close formations on open ground were virtually unstoppable by more lightly armoured opponents. They would just plough through them.' This explains the success of Roman legionaries as well as later Roman-style armoured warriors and dismounted knights in the medieval period. 'In a forest or rough ground, which breaks up formations, armoured men are at a distinct disadvantage. Less aware of what is going on around them, they are far slower to react to more agile lightly armoured troops using spears rather than swords. Panic sets in and

soon armoured groups collapse and run.'

Shadrake remembers a particular occasion when they practised with a rival group who they invited to join them on ground of their own choosing in a forest. 'Early that morning we dug some shallow pits in the ground before our position and then covered these with brushwood. When our rivals advanced, the first rows plunged into the pits and tumbled forward, tripping up the warriors behind them. From being a terrifying, slowly advancing horde, they turned into a surprised muddle and we counter-attacked with our spears to great success.'

One of the great myths of medieval warfare is the power of horsemen over footsoldiers. Armoured knights are supposed to have been able to crash into groups of footsoldiers like tanks, shattering the defenders on impact. In reality, horses do not act like this. They try to avoid collisions and when confronted with a wall of shields and spears, prefer to veer away from it or just stop. 'We had one very fierce horse, used to police work and loud noises,' recalls Shadrake, 'but even he just halted at our shield wall, reared up on two legs and showed us his hooves, nothing more effective than that. Just so long as we stood tight behind our shields we were safe.' What horsemen hoped for was that their mere appearance would unnerve footsoldiers sufficiently to make them run, thus enabling horsemen to outpace and slash down at them from their mounts.

KNIGHTS AND ARCHERS

In Medieval Britain victory in battle was regarded as a sign of divine endorsement. War itself was the pursuit of justice by other means, and kings, noblemen and the common people were prepared to fight for their rights.

The history of medieval Britain is peppered with campaigns, battles and sieges. Kings were repeatedly challenged by powerful nobles. On the battlefield the mounted knight was challenged by the humble, but deadly footsoldier armed with bow and arrows. Kings and barons, knights and archers, were the political and military checks and balances that operated throughout this period. It is perhaps no surprise therefore that the most enduring hero of this period is Robin Hood. Neither a noble or king

English bowman draws an ash arrow across his yew bow. Archers carried several kinds of arrow with different heads, some long and pointed intended to punch through mail, others broad and curved intended to inflict crippling flesh wounds. [Wolfshead Bowmen]

but a yeoman, a member of the free class of ordinary Englishmen of no great wealth or power, Robin Hood is presented through numerous ballads and legends as a good outlaw. With his band of followers, he battles against corrupt officials; he is not opposed to the good king Richard, but violently resentful of bad government. The money he steals from the rich, he gives to the poor, thus establishing a check on bad power. And the base for his actions was the forest.

Ever since William the Conqueror won the English crown at Hastings, the forest has been viewed in Britain as a home for freedom fighters and righteous outlaws. This may stem from the fact that William and the suc-

Gatehouse of Carisbrooke Castle.

Early 13th century knight of the type involved in the murder of St Thomas à Becket at Canterbury. He wears a new form of flat-topped helm with visor. His kite-shaped shield is a later, shorter version of that used by the Normans at Hastings. [John Cole/Conquest]

ceeding Norman kings brought in new laws which sought to turn the forests of England into private estates, reserved for the hunting of game by the king and his loyal knights. The New Forest in Hampshire in southern England is the most well known of these newly established royal estates, being brought under direct royal rule in 1079. Strict laws punished the unauthorised harvesting of the forest's resources by people who had previously considered it their natural right. A sense of this new Norman tyranny of noble huntsmen is conveyed in the Laud Chronicle:

'Many men both saw and heard a great number of huntsmen hunting. The huntsmen were black, huge and hideous, and rode on black horses and on black he-goats and their hounds were jet black, with eyes like saucers and horrible.'

Earlier, in 1086, the same chronicle sums up the rule of William in a poem:

'He caused castles to be built
Which were a sore burden to the poor.
A hard man was the king
And took from his subjects many marks...
He set apart a vast deer preserve and imposed laws concerning it.
Whoever slew a hart or a hind
Was to be blinded.
He forbade the killing of boars
Even as the killing of harts.
For he loved the stags as dearly
As though he had been their father...'
[translation by G.N. Garmonsway, Everyman, 1953]

It is little wonder then that when Robin Hood killed a deer for his followers to eat, it was an act of defiance which made him a hugely popular hero. Finally, and perhaps most importantly for British military history, Robin Hood had as his main weapon not a sword or a lance but a bow. Until the popularity of Robin Hood in tales from the 14th century onwards, the bow had always been the sign of a bad sort in medieval literature. 'Cursed be the first man who became an archer,' wrote the 13th century poet Bertrand de Bar-sur-Aube. 'He was afraid and did not dare approach.' As far as knights were concerned, the only manly way of fighting was with sword and lance. If treachery was suspected in a death, then it was usually claimed to have been delivered by an arrow. In a drawing by Matthew Paris, the king of France is shown unhorsed at Bouvines in 1214 by an arrow, while William Rufus, son of William the Conqueror, was assassinated by an arrow in the head while hunting in the New Forest in 1100.

Previously considered the weapon of the coward, in the hands of Robin Hood the bow became a weapon of freedom, an equaliser against the armoured knight, and it is no surprise that the reputation of this greatest hero of archery should flower in the minds of the English people just at the time of their greatest victories against the French at Crécy (1346), Poitiers (1356), and Agincourt (1415), all of which were victories largely achieved by English archers against French knights. By the 16th century, the bow was a much loved weapon, emblematic of English freedom and retained in the Tudor army long after guns dominated the battlefield.

If Robin Hood and the growing reputation of the archer symbolised individual liberty in medieval Britain, the hard work of limiting royal centralised power was actually achieved during a series of civil wars fought between nobles and the king. None of these was fought for the ideal of political freedom, far from it, they were largely struggles for personal power, but some of the by-products of these conflicts, such as the Magna Carta, added substantially to the rule of law and to checks on the power of the state.

Simon de Montfort was a prime mover in the civil wars of the mid-13th century. Born in France, he was earl of Leicester and a leader of the English barons who protested against the rule of King Henry III. In 1258, these noblemen forced Henry to agree to a plan of reform called the 'Provisions of Oxford', which restricted royal power by

KNIGHTS IN ARMOUR

The age of Edward I saw a transformation in the armour worn by knights and their retainers. The beginning of the 13th century saw the final evolution of the mail shirt. Called a hauberk, it was a long, close-fitting tunic of mail down to the knees with sleeves of mail that included mail mittens as well as separate pieces of mail worn over the legs and feet. A mail hood finished off the complete armour with perhaps a conical helmet with a nasal worn over it, in earlier Norman style, or a completely closed helmet called a helm. A cloth surcoat was worn over the mail and this served as a means of identification being coloured in the heraldry of the family to which the soldier belonged.

By the middle of the 13th century, armourers were experimenting with new forms of armour, namely pieces of steel plate. Rectangular plates called ailettes were attached to the shoulders and protected against downward sword blows. Knees were protected by plates called poleyns. Visors were added to helms so that the knight could open his helmet when not in combat.

Early 12th century knight, typical of the Norman-style warriors that now ruled Britain. He wears a long mail shirt with mail mittens and carries a mace.
[Regia Anglorum]

These developments established a trend that grew in the 14th century. Larger pieces of plate armour were attached to arms and legs over mail. Armoured gauntlets took over from mail mittens. The surcoat was shortened and became known as a gipon. Smaller helmets following the shape of the head came into fashion, either worn by themselves or under the great helm. These were called basinets and had visors added to them later in the 14th century.

It is an old view that knights in armour were ponderous fighters who, if unhorsed, would be useless on the ground and, if knocked over, would flail around like turtles on their backs. Re-enactors have shown that warriors in armour in fact faced no particular problems of weight as both mail and plate armour were designed to distribute the weight over the body. Warriors thus equipped can run and jump and fight with great speed and agility. Problems arise mainly from heat exhaustion, when fighting on a warm day can create excessive heat and sweat under the armour.

John Cole of medieval re-enactment group Conquest describes the experience of fighting in armour:

'Beneath our mail we wear a thick quilted aketon which helps to cushion blows against our armour, but on a warm day it becomes stiflingly hot and we just use a half-strength one. These quilted coats filled with padding could absorb several arrows and warriors must have considered it worth the discomfort.'

The tight fitting mail also prevented completely flexible movements.

'In close combat, mail enclosing the entire arm with mittens as well as mail leggings is highly effective against sword cuts and the sacrifice in movement would have been worth it. In pauses between combat, you can see many of our re-enactor members jumping up and down to loosen the mail which can bunch, or hitching it up so the belt supports its weight on the hips as well as the shoulders. This must have happened in real combat.'

Close-up of mail leggings worn beneath the long mail shirt by 12th century knights. As the century progressed, mail armour was increased to cover every aspect of the body, including hands, feet, and face. [Regia Anglorum]

Members of Conquest re-enactment group recreate an encampment. [John Cole/Conquest]

placing government administration in the hands of 24 barons. A few years later, Henry broke the agreement and compelled the barons, led by Simon de Montfort, to take up arms to assert their authority. It was a reckless act on the part of the king, for Simon de Montfort was a formidable warlord. His father had led the Albigensian Crusade which crushed the Cathars in southern France with exceptional brutality; now Simon embraced this

Barons' War as a crusade also, telling his soldiers to wear white crosses on their tunics as the king 'had broken so many oaths that he had become the enemy of God.'

The two armies met at Lewes in Sussex in 1264. King Henry commanded the central body of his support-ers, while his brother commanded the left flank and his son, Prince Edward, the right flank. Simon de Montfort led an army he had divided into five groups, with one held in reserve. On the morning of the battle, he seized the heights above the town of Lewes, provoking King Henry to attack without any plan, just unleashing his mounted knights led by Prince Edward. Many of de Montfort's supporters were not professional soldiers and his body of Londoners fled before the royal assault. The mounted warriors pursued the fleeing footsoldiers for four miles, giving no quarter, slashing downwards with their great swords, until heaps of bodies littered the battlefield, but Prince Edward's charge had weakened the royal army and de Montfort took prompt action to exploit this. With

a furious attack downhill he pushed the main royalist army back into the city of Lewes and when Prince Edward returned from his pursuit, it was only to join his father as a prisoner.

Simon de Montfort was declared Head of State and in 1265 he established a parliament in which representatives from all the boroughs and cities served alongside the barons and clergy, thus including the Commons for the first time in English government. However, de Montfort's triumph was short-lived, breaking down in acrimony, and Prince Edward eventually led the royalists to victory at the battle of Evesham. King Henry was restored to the throne, his power restricted, and the court was dominated by Prince Edward who became King Edward I in 1272.

A period of strong monarchy and government stability ensued, enabling England to look beyond its frontiers and become for the first time an imperial power, thus beginning a new phase in its military history. In Wales, Llywellyn tested Edward's resolve. In a letter to the English king, the Welsh prince wrote:

'We have received a letter written in the King's name. It forbids us to build a castle on our own land. We are sure it was not written with your knowledge and would not have

Knight in full plate armour. The final development in medieval armour occurred in the 15th century when plate armour took over completely from mail, producing some of the most complex and beautiful suits of armour ever made. [Philipp Elliot-Wright/English Heritage]

Recreated 12th century knight stands before Rochester Castle, a typical Norman-style keep built in the 12th century. The knight wears a coloured surcoat and helmet indicating his military allegiance. A high-sided wooden saddle keeps him upright and allows him to charge with a lance couched beneath his arm. [Regia Anglorum]

been sent if you had been in the country, for you know well that the rights of our principality are totally separate from the rights of your kingdom. We and our ancestors have long had the power within our boundaries to build castles without prohibition by any one.'

It was a slap in the face to the new King Edward.

Edward called Llywellyn's bluff. The Welsh prince expected the usual disunity between English nobility and Crown to prevent a major campaign. But in 1277 Edward led an army into northern Wales and it was Llywellyn's forces that suffered from disunity. His Welsh allies deserted him for Edward. Llywellyn was forced to make homage to Edward, but he remained prince of his realm.

Five years later, Welsh resentment boiled over. Rebels burned English estates. In response, Edward ordered a many-pronged attack, incorporating the Marcher lords in the south and centre of Wales and his own army in the north. Llywellyn was killed in a skirmish with a Marcher lord. His head was cut off and sent to Edward, who had it placed on a spear at the Tower of London. For the first time in its history, Wales was now under the direct control of the English. An ancient crown was uncovered, supposedly belonging to the legendary king Arthur, and this was presented to King Edward's son who became Prince of Wales. The Welsh were furious, Arthur was a Celtic hero and they claimed he remained in the mountains of Wales, awaiting his time to triumph over the enemies of his people. The English responded by uncovering the supposed bones of the dead Arthur on English soil at Glastonbury. Having stolen the land of the Celts, the English had also

stolen their hero.

It was during Edward's campaigns in Wales that we first become aware of Welsh archers as a distinct military element. Giraldus Cambrensis, a century earlier, had remarked on their natural skills of archery.

'William de Braose testifies that one of his warriors was wounded by a Welsh arrow which passed through his mail clad thigh, his saddle, and penetrated his horse. Another knight has his armoured hip pierced by an arrow to the saddle. When he turned round, he received another arrow through his leg which fixed him to his horse. Yet the bows used by the Welsh are not made of horn, ivory, or yew [like powerful composite bows used elsewhere in Europe], but of wild elm. They are unpolished and rough, yet stout.'

This was not the 'longbow', which in truth never existed in the Middle Ages, but a simple wooden bow. It was not so much the weapon that was important but the way the archers were employed. Edward initiated this by using Welsh archers not in ambushes, as they had been used to fighting, but to disrupt formations of cavalry and footsoldiers at longer ranges. It was this tactic, performed by Welsh mercenaries, that Edward took with him to Scotland on his next imperial challenge.

The wars between Scotland and England in the late 13th and early 14th centuries have often been portrayed as a national struggle for freedom, but the reality was far different. The majority of nobles who ruled estates in Scotland and northern England were Anglo-Norman, descendants of William the Conqueror's knights. The ordinary people who served on these estates may have been Celtic-speaking, but they owed their alle-

BOWS VERSUS CROSSBOWS

Edward I made great use of large groups of Welsh archers in his wars against the Scots. His grandson, Edward III, took substantial numbers of Welsh and English archers with him to France where they won stunning victories over armies of French knights. This established the legend of British archery as one of the most potent massed weapons of the medieval period. It is a curious success because the bow or longbow as it later became known was itself not an especially impressive weapon.

The 'longbow' did not exist in medieval vocabulary; it was simply called a bow. What is today identified as a longbow is based on the Victorian sporting bow which was christened by manufacturers who saw a good sales pitch by identifying it with the bows of English legend. The 14th century bow, as far as it can be reconstructed, was a simple wooden weapon, certainly not as powerful as the composite bow which was widely available in Europe and combined the power of wood with animal sinew and horn.

The crossbow, usually associated with foreign mercenaries, was a composite bow with the added power of a mechanical device that created even greater tension in the string than mere arm power could achieve. This was the most powerful form of bow in Europe and could be devastating when fired by a mass of crossbowmen.

The supposed advantage of the wooden bow is that it was both cheap and easy to use. Nevertheless, it still required considerable skill to use effectively. An archer armed with a bow was supposed to have a speed advantage over the crossbowman because it takes longer to pull back the string on a crossbow, but practical experience shows that two crossbowmen working together, one pulling the string and the other shooting, can achieve a high rate of firepower too. Medieval illustrations show crossbowmen working in teams of two. Rather than being aimed, the crossbow, like the bow, would be pointed into the air so its bolt dropped from the sky like a mini-missile. Why medieval crossbowmen could charge more for their services than other archers is somewhat of a mystery, although they probably had to account for the initial cost of the crossbow, which would be more expensive than the ordinary bow, and also, no doubt, there was a degree of professional mystification added to the deal.

top: Row of recreated 14th century archers of the type that proved so devastating during the Hundred Years War when massed ranks of English and Welsh bowmen defeated the finest French knights at Crécy and Poitiers. [Philipp Elliot-Wright/English Heritage]

right: North and east towers of Pevensey Castle.

opposite: Crossbow. A composite bow with a trigger, it was more powerful than the so-called longbow.

giance to their lord and their clan, not a modern notion of nationhood which did not exist at the time. Thus, when Alexander III, King of the Scots, died without an heir in 1286, it was two Anglo-Norman nobles who contested the right to succeed him and they asked Edward I, as feudal superior, to decide. Edward chose John Balliol, thus alienating the other contestant, Robert Bruce.

Edward proceeded to overplay his hand and Balliol tired of being a puppet-king. Edward led an army north and crushed him at Dunbar. An English viceroy was appointed instead of Balliol. As a further sign of dominance, Edward had the sacred stone of Scone, upon which generations of Scottish kings had been crowned, removed and taken to Westminster Abbey where it remained until recently. Opposition in Scotland was then championed by the legendary William Wallace. Harassed by English tax collectors, Wallace surrounded himself with outlaw warriors. Surprised one evening by an English patrol, he took cover in his woman's house. The English burnt the house, Wallace escaped, but his lover died in the flames. Wallace vowed vengeance.

Several Scots nobles raised their banners in support of Wallace. Robert Bruce was asked by Edward to quell the revolt, but he joined

inset: Reconstruction of Restormel Castle showing the typical motte and bailey construction of early Norman castles with a mound and enclosure.
[Drawing by T. Ball/English Heritage]

Early 12th century knights assault a castle, recreated by re-enactment group Regia Anglorum. This was a notorious period of conflict, the protracted civil war between King Stephen and Matilda, both claimants for the English throne. Finally, Henry II, Matilda's son, emerged as a strong king, establishing the Plantagenet dynasty.
[Regia Anglorum]

the rebels too. Edward sent his lieutenant John de Warenne to Scotland and in 1297 the two forces clashed on a bridge crossing the river Forth north of Stirling. Wallace waited for half the knights to cross the bridge, then attacked while some of his men broke down the bridge itself. Armoured knights floundered in the waterlogged fields of the riverbank while Scots armed with spears and axes pulled and prodded them from their horses. When the bridge collapsed, the English vanguard was isolated and slaughtered. Among the dead was Hugh de Cressingham, chief tax collector for King Edward in Scotland. Wallace had the tax collector's body flayed and a broad strip of his skin made into a belt for his sword.

Edward I was forced to return from campaigning in France to deal with Wallace, now knighted by Robert Bruce and proclaimed Guardian of the Kingdom of Scotland. Based at York, Edward recruited a professional army of mercenaries alongside his loyalist knights. With some 12,000 footsoldiers and 2,500 horsemen, Edward cornered Wallace at Falkirk. In traditional Scots style, Wallace took a defensive position against the English cavalry and drew his spearmen into tight formations. The English knights scattered the Scots horsemen, but failed to dislodge the spearmen. Edward called them back from disaster and instead handed the battle to his Welsh archers who now stood from afar and rained a hail of arrows on the Scots footsoldiers. Unable to move, the Scots fell beneath the arrows, weakening their formations. It was then that Edward sent his horsemen back into the conflict and shattered Scots resistance. Wallace escaped but his power had vanished with his army.

In 1305, William Wallace was betrayed by some of his own countrymen and taken to London where he was dragged through the streets, hanged and dismembered. The next year, Robert Bruce proclaimed himself king of Scotland. English forces hounded him, but in 1307 as Edward I prepared a major campaign against him, the English king died. Before he died, however, Edward had extracted from his son a promise to carry on the war with Bruce and another promise to carry Edward's coffin ahead of his army into Scotland. Edward II was no great warrior like his father and it took several years until he felt ready to carry out his father's dying wish.

In 1314, Edward II advanced to the relief of Stirling, where the garrison was committed to surrender if the siege was not broken by midsummer's day. Edward's army was substantial: 500 knights, 2,000 other horsemen, 3,000 Welsh archers, and up to 15,000 foot-soldiers. Robert Bruce was outnumberd, the core of his army consisting of 5,000 spearmen from all over Scotland, both lowlanders and highlanders, plus a few archers and some 500 horsemen. It did not look promising; it was the same kind of force that had been devastated at Falkirk. The chosen battleground was near a little stream called Bannock. Bruce chose a defensive position, digging pits which he covered with brushwood.

On the morning of the battle Robert Bruce was in the open ground between the two armies, surveying the situation, when an English knight, Sir Humphry de Bohun, recognised him and charged. A commander should sensibly have avoided the challenge and retreated, but Bruce could not do this in full view of his men and urged his horse on to the duel. The knight's lance deflected off Bruce's armour and the Scots king raised himself in his stirrups and brought his battleaxe crashing down on the English knight's helmet, splitting open his head. The Scots gave a

Skirmish between 12th century knights. Most early medieval illustrations, including the famous Bayeux Tapestry, show armoured warriors using lances and spears overarm for both stabbing and throwing. [Philipp Elliot-Wright/English Heritage]

Two knights of the early 12th century, recreated by medieval re-enactment group Conquest, clash in close combat. They wear the long sleeved mail hauberk with hood which was the most popular form of armour at the time. [John Cole/Conquest]

14th century knights practice combat at a recreated tournament. Knights now wear both mail and plate armour as well as the magnificent great helms which offered superb protection but also limited awareness of the battlefield. [Medieval Combat Society]

great cheer and charged forward.

This time, the Scots spears proved effective and the English knights and cavalry could do little to break the schiltron formations. Nightfall eventually brought the clash to an end, but the battle had not been decided and both armies waited through the long summer night. In the morning, the Scots left their defensive positions and rolled down the hillside in three densely packed phalanxes. Edward's knights surged forward to meet the spearmen, preventing the archers from supporting them. Axes cracked on armour and spears broke through mail. It was a ferocious hand to hand combat with the English forced slowly back to the boggy ground around the Bannock stream. Collapsing into the water, English nerves finally broke and Edward's knights grabbed his reins and led him away from the disaster.

Northern England was raided and Robert Bruce sent his brother to Ireland to conquer the Anglo-Irish and unite the countries. But English forces returned to Scotland and the Irish campaign ended in defeat for Bruce and his allies. However, Edward II had more dangerous enemies at home and was ultimately overthrown and murdered. Wales erupted in rebellion. It was fortunate for England that Edward III took control of the throne and proved a soldier of tremendous ability in the style of his grandfather. He turned his attention to France and his claims on that kingdom. This conflict, which came to be known as the Hundred Years War, is best remembered for three of the greatest victories in English medieval history: Crécy, Poitiers and Agincourt.

The wars of Edward I and Edward III are notable for being fought on a greater scale than those before and after them. For his wars in Wales and Scotland Edward I gathered armies 30,000 strong, some three times larger than the average force in earlier medieval warfare. These was more like armies of the late 16th century. Although based around feudal dues of loyalty and service owed by leading noblemen who gained from the patronage of the Crown, the majority of soldiers in these larger armies were paid for; they included foreign mercenaries as well as soldiers recruited from Wales and England. Such large armies required complex organisation, especially of supplies: wheat, barley, oats, beans, salt fish, beef and bacon were provided by a network of local authorities and tradesmen, bringing supplies into major base towns such as Chester, Berwick and Carlisle. Edward I and his government must have been supreme administrators and effective tax collectors to organise such campaigns.

The armies of Edward I could not rely on feudal allegiance and the possibility of battlefield loot alone. They had to be paid and this required more money than had ever been required before in British warfare. Edward's first Welsh war cost around £20,000, that of 1282-4 cost near enough £150,000. Edward III's campaigns in France from 1369 to 1375 are estimated to have cost £670,000. Where did this money come from?

Parliament was a useful tool for raising taxes and Edward I must have enjoyed its support for between 1294 and 1297, £190,000 of tax was raised. It also indicates that the tax revenue system must have been efficient, if not ruthless, in imposing this demand on the English people and collecting the money voted by parliament. Indirect taxes in the form of custom duties were also profitable; English exports of wool and hides to Europe were enjoying a boom. Finally, the arrival of Italian bankers in the City of London enabled the king to raise massive loans from the likes of the Riccardi of Lucca and the Frescobaldi of Florence. Unfortunately, the repayment relationship between Crown and bank was not always good and several financiers went bankrupt, with the Riccardi being owed £392,000 in 1294.

Not only did Edward I possess the money to employ larger armies; he also embarked on a military building scheme of which a series of castles in Wales are the best examples. Norman castles had been relatively simple fortresses based around a central, square stone keep raised on a mound and surrounded by a wall and ditch. Edward's castles were enormous, complex buildings in which round towers sprouted from several rings of tall battlements. The keep was abandoned in favour of a concentric design in which two or three lines of defence ran around a central space or bailey. The round or multi-faceted towers projected from the walls to give greater arcs of fire, with archers aiming through window slits at attackers. At Caernarvon Castle, the towers rise to different heights and can be defended independently. At Harlech Castle, the massive gatehouse boasted three great doors and three portcullises. Beaumaris Castle, the last of Edward's Welsh bastions, has inner and outer curtain walls with the inner walls being taller and thus adding an extra layer of defence to the outside ring. A water-filled moat provides yet another layer of defence. The labour and materials as well as the design complexity involved in all these major building projects indicates that a new level of military capability had been reached in Britain.

Rochester Castle seen from Rochester cathedral, is a splendid example of a Norman stone keep. [English Heritage]

TUDORS
AND GUNS

*Thirty years of civil war, known as The Wars of the Roses
established Britain with a new royal dynasty, the Tudors.
Within another generation, the appearance of portable
firearms transformed the way battles were fought.*

The initial impact of gunpowder on British warfare was all but unnoticed. It arrived in the form of an obscure recipe, probably copied from an Arabic source. Albertus Magnus made a copy of the Liber Igneum or 'Book of Explosives' and passed it on to his pupil Roger Bacon, a

English officer at the time of the Spanish Armada in 1588, recreated by a member of English Renaissance. Armies depended much more on firepower by the end of the 16th century, whether it be field artillery and massed ranks of arquebusiers, or ships mounted with huge cannons, although in the case of the defeat of the Spanish Armada, it was the weather that played the decisive part. [English Renaissance]

Franciscan monk and amateur scientist. Bacon's enquiries into the ways of the world trod on sensitive ground, as far as the church was concerned, so he had to disguise his scientific writings in opaque language but in 1242, he recorded the following combination: 'Of saltpetre take 7 parts, 5 of young hazel-twigs [in the form of charcoal], and 5 of sulphur; and so thou wilt call up thunder and destruction.'

Rockets and weapons that exploded were already known in China and used by the Mongols. It appears that this was how gunpowder was first employed in Britain. There is a reference to 'crakys of war' used by Edward III in a campaign against the Scots. The idea of the gun or cannon evolved only slowly. An English manuscript of 1327 portrays a vase-shaped weapon lying on its side with an armoured soldier using a lighted taper to ignite the gunpowder which fires a large arrow from the open end of the vase. By 1346, Edward III was impressed sufficiently by the performance of these primitive weapons to take several with him to France. These early cannons were relatively small, made of wrought iron bars bound with iron hoops and mounted on wooden carts. The size of cannons increased throughout the 14th century until one used at the siege of Aberystwyth weighed in at 4,480lbs and fired a massive stone ball. Edinburgh Castle's famous Mons Meg could throw a 20 inch iron ball almost a mile. These weapons could now play a useful part in battering castle walls, alongside other siege engines, but they were still not battle winners.

One of the most important steps in the use of gunpowder occurred some time in the middle of the 15th century. Previously, the three main ingredients of gunpowder were pounded separately into powders and then mixed together. During transport, the dry mixture might separate and end up in different strengths according to whatever was scooped out of the gunpowder barrel, resulting in a variety of effects when ignited. With the invention of a wet mix technique, gunpowder's performance became more reliable. Saltpetre was dissolved in water and allowed to percolate into charcoal. The active ingredient now resided within the charcoal and, when dried, it was squeezed through sieves to produce a powder of uniform grain size. This resulted in a more dependable explosive reaction. Firing tests with recreated medieval guns have shown that guns loaded with 14th century dry-mix powder misfired once in every four shots, whereas a gun using 15th century wet-mix powder misfired one time in ten. Firing a steel bullet at steel armour, one tenth of an inch thick, a wet-mix gun penetrated five times out of eight, whereas a dry-

mix gun failed to penetrate at all.

With this revolution in gunpowder, guns made a greater impact on the battlefield. The power of French artillery in the mid-15th century is partly credited for ending the Hundred Years War in favour of the French. Also, hand cannons or handguns had until then been a mere novelty whereas, by the end of the 15th century, they had become firearms and would be the most dominant weapon on the 16th century battlefield. In Britain, however, the gun revolution was slow. Long into the 16th century the British retained a reverence for the bow, with archers still employed

Reconstruction of an Elizabethan cannon of the type awaiting the Spanish Armada in 1588.

RISE AND FALL OF ARMOUR

During the Wars of the Roses, in the late 15th century, body armour reached its highest development. Mail, once the most dominant of medieval forms of armour, was now a secondary element, used to fill in gaps between a suit of armour made completely out of shaped pieces of metal plate. Numerous little pieces of plate were strapped and riveted together to form a wholly flexible suit of armour that covered the body from head to toe, much like the segmented armour seen in nature on a lobster or crab. Although it looked powerful and solid, it weighed little more than a coat of mail and no more than the full kit worn by a 20th century soldier, the weight of the armour being distributed over the body. It was not solely the preserve of mounted knights either, but professional paid warriors called men-at-arms frequently fought on foot in full armour.

Current research suggests that these completely armoured men-at-arms may have fought in teams with more lightly armoured retainers who could look out for each other. Recreating warfare of the late 15th century, says Mark Fry of The White Company group of re-enactors, has led us to several new conclusions.

'The most natural formation for armoured soldiers fighting on foot is to be surrounded by their retainers, the men who would have served them in civilian life, car-

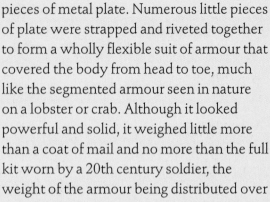

Knight in full suit of plate armour. His helmet is an Italian form of the open basinet called a barbuta and appears to be based on ancient Greek helmets of a similar shape. Although his armour could have been made in England, its clean curved surfaces are typical of Italian armour which was exported all over Europe. The other great style of armour in the late 15th century was the heavily fluted armour known as Gothic and made in southern Germany. [Philipp Elliot-Wright/English Heritage]

Two medieval knights, recreated by the Ragged Staff Medieval Society, fight on foot with swords. Despite the impact of guns and archery, fully-armoured knights were still an important aspect of any late medieval battle, although increased firepower meant is was safer for them to fight on foot rather than on horseback. [Lynda Woodhouse]

rying on this social contract into battle. These retainers would have been lightly armoured but carried bills and pole-arms. They would cluster behind their armoured lords who would function as centres of combat, battering through lightly armed troops, something like human tanks. But full armour prevents complete vision on the battlefield and some agility is lost, so the less armoured retainers would look out for them, picking them up if they fell, protecting their flanks. A natural master and servant relationship.'

Frequently added to these combat groups would be a single armoured man carrying a handgun.

'It seems unlikely they served in formations like later musketeers, but acted more as anti-tank guns, being an individual part of the battle clump, advancing close to the opposing armoured man-at-arms and blasting him at close range, thus disabling one whole group of warriors.'

There were two principal styles of armour worn by English knights and men-at-arms in the 15th century, both coming from abroad. Northern Italy and Southern Germany were major areas of arms manu-

Armoured knight with a two-handed sword. By the time of the Wars of the Roses, mail armour had been largely overtaken by plate armour, which proved more effective against arrows and gunshot. The fluting on the armour is highly decorative but also helped to create a surface that might deflect any indirect fire. [Lynda Woodhouse]

facture in the Middle Ages and they developed two distinct forms of armour. The German style is now known as Gothic and was composed of numerous fluted plates giving a spiky silhouette to the overall figure. The flutes had a purpose beyond decoration in that they provided further glancing surfaces to reduce the impact of weapons. Italian armour was simpler with less fussy shapes and plain surfaces but equally well designed to create glancing forms as well. These types of armour were either imported into Britain or copied by English armourers who added their own variations. Only the wealthiest knights could afford entire new suits of armour, especially if imported, but various pieces of armour were worn by men-at-arms and their more lightly armoured retainers who might wear a breastplate with tassets to protect the thighs, perhaps some armour for the arms and a helmet of the new style such as a Gothic sallet with flaring neckguard and slit visor. Thickly padded jackets called

gambesons were also popular among more humble soldiers and archers who did not expect to be in the thick of combat.

By the early 16th century, handguns in the form of the more efficient arquebus, were making a considerable impact on the battlefield, but this only slowly reduced the amount of armour worn. Even though a breastplate could not stand up to a well directed blast of shot without being made too heavy and thick to wear, it could still serve a purpose in combat, protecting against indirect firepower and pikes and swords. Also, aristocratic warriors and their retainers were loathe to give up a form of armour that reinforced their social status and thus, ironically, some of the most beautiful suits of armour were created during this twilight period, utilising many of the classical motifs of the Renaissance. With the introduction of the musket at the end of the 16th century, many warriors finally gave up their armour in return for greater agility and awareness of the battlefield. That said, the breastplate and helmet remained a favourite of pikemen involved in close hand-to-hand combat and some cavalry who fought with swords and lances as well as pistols.

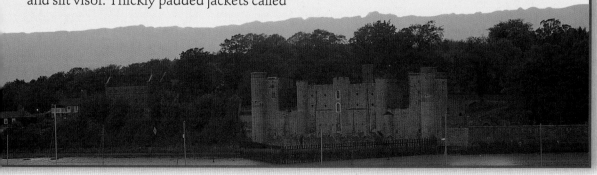

alongside soldiers armed with the new arquebus or matchlock gun.

The collapse of British power in France reflected a failure of leadership. The glory days of Edward III were long gone and several noble factions competed to rule England, chief among them the Houses of Lancaster and York, represented (retrospectively) by a red rose and a white rose. The Wars of the Roses wracked England for thirty years from 1455 to 1485 as the two rival dynastic families battled for supremacy. Defeat in France destabilised the political situation in England. News of French victories forcing English settlers out of Normandy and Bordeaux, regions that had been under English rule for centuries, stirred up discontent.

In 1450, an Irish ex-soldier called Jack Cade raised the men of Kent in a rebellion that led to fighting in the streets of London. The Lord Treasurer was decapitated in a pub, the mob stormed the Tower of London, and a pitched battle took place on London Bridge, before order was restored. In 1453, the year of final defeat in France, the Lancastrian King Henry VI was declared insane and the duke of York became Protector. Two years later, the king recovered, his family and the duke's enemies combining to restore him to the throne.

Many of the nobles and professional soldiers who took part in this conflict were veterans of the wars in France. They brought a new, murderous efficiency to warfare in Britain. 'Their fathers and their followers pillaged and

Medieval crossbowman recreated by a member of The White Company. The crossbow was superior in firepower to the ordinary bow, but the English have always regarded it as a foreign weapon and it has consequently been denigrated, although large numbers of crossbowmen, usually foreign mercenaries, were employed during the Wars of the Roses. [Jill Perry]

destroyed the kingdom of France,' wrote Philippe de Commynes at the end of the 15th century, 'but they all killed each other.'

The opening round of the Wars of the Roses began when King Henry VI dismissed Richard duke of York from his position as Protector. Richard joined forces with, among others, Richard Neville earl of Warwick, and retaliated by claiming the throne for himself. The Lancastrians won the first round: the duke of York was killed in battle, his son Edmund executed for good measure. However, his eldest son Edward took over the Yorkist cause and proclaimed himself Edward IV. Welcomed into London by the pro-Yorkist citizens, he pursued the Lancastrians north. On 28 March 1461 they turned to fight at Towton.

Edward's army is said to have totalled some 36,000 men and included in its van-guard, led by Lord Fauconberg, his own followers from Kent as well as soldiers from the Welsh borders. Edward commanded the main body which included a substantial number of Burgundian mercenaries, some armed with handguns. The Lancastrian army of perhaps 40,000 was under the command of the Duke of Somerset. Both armies were unlikely to have been as large as the chroniclers would have us believe; all that can be said with confidence is that Towton was the biggest battle contemporaries had experienced.

The Lancastrian army was camped north of the river Aire between the villages of Saxton and Towton, 15 miles south-west of York. It was bitterly cold and sleet drove across the battlefield. Skirmishing revolved around possession of a bridge over the river Aire; Fauconberg sent archers mounted on

Medieval archer recreated by a member of The White Company. Archers were used during the Wars of the Roses in mass formations, delivering artillery-like barrages at the beginning of a battle. [Jill Perry]

horseback to cross where the water was shallow, the rapid movement caught the Lancastrians off guard and inflicted many casualties. Edward crossed the river with his main force and on 29 March, with snow blowing in the faces of his warriors, he advanced towards the Lancastrian position half a mile south of Towton village.

Henry VI remained in York, the fate of his dynasty in Somerset's hands. Around 9 o'clock, the wind changed direction and Fauconberg ordered his archers forward to take advantage of the extra range the wind gave them. The Lancastrian archers replied with their own volleys but their arrows fell

Recreated Scots archers and pikemen advance across the battlefield of Flodden Field where the English army defeated the Scots in 1513. The battle was fought as part of the Auld Alliance between France and Scotland, but with the death of some 10,000 Scots and their king, many wondered whether the alliance was worth pursuing. [English Renaissance]

short, Faunconberg ordered his archers forward to pick up the Lancastrian arrows and launch them back. Under this demoralising arrow shower, Somerset ordered his army to attack. The greater number of Lancastrian warriors caused the Yorkist line to wobble under their impact, but inspired by the presence of Edward in the fighting mass alongside them, the Yorkists exchanged blow for blow, sword and axe clanging against halberd and warhammer.

Both sides were ordered not to give quarter; wounded or surrendering soldiers were dispatched without mercy. A force of Lancastrians emerged from Castle Hill Wood on the Yorkist left flank, but the Yorkists committed their reserves. It was now the middle of the afternoon and both sides must

have been exhausted with the physical effort of fighting in armour, the only good thing about the cold weather being that it reduced their body heat.

Edward could see his men being pushed back and back and must have wondered if all was lost until a body of new troops arrived led by the duke of Norfolk. This proved the decisive factor. These fresh warriors forced the tired Lancastrians back until eventually their line broke and they fled in panic. Lancastrian soldiers tumbled down the snowy slopes of the river Cock behind them, many died in the crush or drowned in the icy waters. The area became known ever after as the Bloody Meadow.

Word went out that all the Lancastrian nobles should be eliminated rather than ransomed. 'In this battle,' wrote George Neville, Bishop of Exeter, 'eleven lords of the enemy fell, including the earl of Devon, the earl of Northumberland, Lord Clifford and Neville with some knights. And from what we hear from persons worthy of confidence, some 28,000 persons perished on one side and the other.' It was ruthless political extermination and the prize for Edward IV was that Henry VI fled to Scotland, allowing him ten years of uninterrupted rule.

In 1470, Edward IV fell out with the earl of Warwick, and, outmanoeuvred, fled to Flanders with his younger brother Richard. Henry VI was released from prison in the Tower of London and replaced on the throne. Warwick was now 'the king-maker', but Edward secured the support of the duke of

Burgundy and returned to Britain with an army of mercenaries. In 1471 at the battle of Barnet, Edward confronted Warwick on a battlefield shrouded in fog. Each right flank enveloped the other until the fighting armies twisted round. In the confusion Lancastrian forces attacked their own men from the rear and cries of treachery led to a rout in which Warwick was killed. Edward consolidated his grip on power with a second victory at Tewkesbury where Henry VI's son and heir was conveniently killed. The unfortunate Henry VI was murdered in the Tower of London on Edward's orders.

Edward IV died prematurely in 1483 and his brother, Richard duke of Gloucester, usurped the throne. Richard III probably murdered Edward's teenage sons in the

Recreated medieval soldiers armed with various forms of polearms or bills. Billmen, fighting in tight formations, were the English version of the pike phalanxes employed so successfully by the Swiss. Such formations could defend themselves against cavalry and were used to break enemy lines. [Philipp Elliot-Wright/English Heritage]

King Henry VIII on board Henri Grace à Dieu bound for France to meet King Francis I on the Field of the Cloth of Gold in June 1520, painting by Volpi. Under the Tudors, Britain discovered the value of seapower and began to expand its navy with the addition of major battleships. [Peter Newark's Military Pictures]

Tower of London, but he never had time to consolidate his grip on power. Henry Tudor earl of Richmond invaded from France in 1485. His claim to the throne was a distant one, but he had 3,000 French mercenaries to back it, and some support in Wales and the West Country. More crucially, Richard had been reduced to taking hostages to compel the loyalty of the powerful Stanley family. When the two armies met at Bosworth, Lord Stanley failed to commit his men to battle, then intervened on the side of his step-son, Henry Tudor. Richard fought bravely, attempting to kill Henry in person, but died in the attempt. According to tradition, Richard's crown was picked up and placed on Henry's head by Lord Stanley.

Crowned Henry VII, Henry Tudor faced a succession of revolts, his repression of potential opposition possibly contributing to the very unrest he sought to quell. His son suc-

ceeded to the throne peacefully, but arbitrary imprisonment and judicial murder were routine tools of Henry VIII's government.

Henry VIII revived the traditional English pursuit of campaigning against France. This called into play the 'Auld Alliance' between France and Scotland. While Henry led his army to France, James IV of Scotland launched an invasion of England. The defence of the north was entrusted to the aged earl of Surrey, who intercepted the Scots at Flodden moor, near Branxton on 9 September 1513. The Scots army took up a defensive position trusting to its ranks of pikemen. The English, as in previous centuries, harassed these formations with long-range archery, as well as with new field artillery, and the impatient Scots eventually attacked. The English resisted the assault and bloodily fought back until James IV was himself killed and thousands of Scots lay dead.

The Mary Rose, depicted in the inventory of Henry VIII's ships. Commissioned in 1511, it was the King's first great warship. Sunk in the Solent in 1545, it was recently raised from the sea and can now be seen in Portsmouth. [Peter Newark's Military Pictures]

Later in the century, English forces inflicted two more crushing victories on the Scots and after the battle of Pinkie in 1547, an English army occupied Edinburgh. By 1585, the Scots had abandoned their alliance with France and signed a treaty with England.

Although largely successful in his French adventures, Henry VIII was shaken by an attempted invasion of England in 1545 when French troops landed at Seaford and the Isle of Wight. The French navy had won temporary dominance of the Channel and it was only the outbreak of dysentery in the French fleet that prevented a successful invasion of England. The experience was a timely reminder for Henry of the need to maintain naval supremacy. He had already overseen innovative shipbuilding at the beginning of

his reign with the launch of the Mary Rose, the first ship to be designed with cannons firing through ports cut in the side of the ship rather than being placed in castles at either end. The remains of this ship were famously recovered and are now on view at Portsmouth. By 1514, Henry had over 30 battle ships, with his flagship being the massive Henri Grace à Dieu. New dockyards and naval storehouses were established from the Thames, including Deptford, Woolwich and Chatham, all along the south coast to Portsmouth. Government expenditure on the navy spiralled. Some £18,824 was spent in just six months in 1547 at the main dockyard of Deptford and a ship list of 1548 shows at least 52 vessels at the King's command.

To protect the southern coast a chain of

TESTING EARLY GUNS

Handguns from the 16th century are very fragile and valuable today and so they are rarely tested to check their performance, but a recent test-firing was carried out by Dr. Peter Krenn at the Styrian Provincial Armoury in Graz in Austria, giving an idea of the impact of firepower in Tudor Britain. A matchlock arquebus of the 1580s was found to penetrate wood to a depth of 19 centimetres at a range of 100 metres. At the same range, it penetrated steel plate to 0.4 centimetres. Its probability of hitting a tar-get at a 100 metres was just over fifty per cent. A modern assault rifle in comparison penetrates wood to a depth of 29 centimetres and steel to 0.9 centimetres over the same range and is, of course, a hundred per cent accurate. The bullet velocity of the arquebus at 30 metres is 470 metres per second and at 100 metres 349 metres per second. The modern assault rifle is approximately twice that. However, considering that there is a difference of four centuries of science between

Woman with medieval handgun.

the two, the primitive arquebus could certainly deliver a considerable impact at a short range.

Beyond a 100 metres or so, the effectiveness of the arquebus dropped significantly, owing to the poor ballistic qualities of large-calibre bullets (in this case 2.2 centimetres), reinforcing the view that most battles were fought at very close range. A test with a wheel-lock pistol of 1620 against a 0.3 centimetre thick breastplate of 1570, fired at a distance of 8.5 metres, shows that the bullet penetrated the armour, but its velocity was reduced so much by the energy needed to punch through the steel that it barely dented the sandbag behind it, thus showing why breastplates were still worn into the 17th century. They could still save your life in close quarter fighting.

Recreated medieval soldier about to trigger an early handgun. Guns such as this, essentially a primitive form of the matchlock arquebus, were surprisingly effective, firing a large calibre bullet which at close-range could be devastating. They were either aimed from the shoulder or fired from the hip. [Jill Perry]

fortresses was built at Sandgate, Deal, Walmer, Dover, the Isle of Wight, Pendennis and St Mawes. These differed from medieval castles by providing openings for cannons behind thick walls and wide ditches that reduced the profile of the fort vulnerable to gunfire. Henry employed a German, Stefan van Haschenperg, to design them, but it was not until the 1560s that truly innovative forms of artillery fortification arrived from the continent such as the fort at Berwick, designed like the star-shaped fortresses pioneered in Italy, using low angled bastions to reduce the impact of incoming shot as well as providing flanking fire to sweep the ditches in front of the walls.

While some European powers recruited substantial forces of soldiers, Queen Elizabeth chose to rely on the militia rather than maintain an expensive standing army. Landowners called upon their tenants and other residents to perform some form of military duty in defence of their district. It was a vestige of feudalism and the days of the yeoman archer; efficiency differed from county to county. In wealthier areas such as London, some serious military preparation was undertaken; there, the 'trained bands' were well armed and versed in military affairs.

County musters were usually organised by a Lord Lieutenant, who, though officially unpaid for his duty, could receive a good income from bribes received for exemptions bought by local men who wished not to serve. Most of the cost of these little armies was met out of local taxation or the patronage of wealthy nobles. When war with Spain became likely after 1585, the government chose not to recruit these good county men for its army, arguing that their absence abroad would dislocate local affairs. Instead, the government ordered Lord Lieutenants to gather vagabonds and men without responsibilities: cannon fodder. The government was accused of scouring the country for criminals and sending them abroad, bringing the reputation of army service into poor repute.

The lack of professional military experience in Britain at this time meant that the use of firearms spread slowly. When Henry VIII invaded France in 1544, only seven per cent of his soldiers were armed with arquebuses, when at least a third of the French army had guns. A great many English soldiers were still armed with the bow, partly because it was cheap and partly because of its association with the great English victories of the past over the French. Henry VIII showed his affection for the bow by practising with it and passing legislation discouraging the use of crossbows and firearms. That said, English monarchs were realistic enough to see that both pike and arquebus were the weapons of the future. When conflict loomed later in the century, the proportion of men armed with these weapons increased.

The arquebus was a match-lock weapon in which a lighted cord ignited the gunpowder in the barrel. By the end of the 16th century, the musket, a larger and heavier weapon that used more gunpowder to blast a ball further with greater impact, was devised. Men armed with long pikes protected the musketeers from cavalry. When volleys of fire had been delivered, both pikemen and musketeers, using their guns like clubs, then advanced to fight in close combat.

Henry VIII broke with Rome in his efforts to sire a legitimate son, appointing himself head of the church in England. In the reign of Elizabeth I, England became a Protestant nation. Her support for rebellious Protestants in the Netherlands incurred the enmity of Spain which controlled a global empire with possessions from Peru to the Philippines. At his great palace of El Escorial, Philip II of Spain slept in a modest bedroom next door to an enormous chapel. He was the armoured fist of the Catholic church and considered any war with Protestants a crusade akin to

English cannon of the type employed at the end of the 16th century explodes into action. If Spanish troops had landed in England, they would have had to deal with firepower such as this employed by both the regular army and the enormous numbers of militiamen raised to meet the threat. [Philipp Elliot-Wright/English Heritage]

15th century cannon recreated by the Ragged Staff Medieval Society. The wrought-iron barrel was mounted on a static carriage and carried to the battlefield. Only later, in the 16th century, were wheels added to the carriage to create mobile artillery. The gunner can be seen loading the pan of the cannon with gunpowder from a powder horn. [Lynda Woodhouse]

fighting his usual enemy, the Turks. The Spanish king was primarily concerned with the Netherlands, where wealthy Dutch towns had revolted against his authority and declared themselves a Protestant republic. Elizabeth sent aid to the Dutch and allowed raids against Spanish ships and ports, led principally by Sir Francis Drake. Philip was provoked into planning an invasion.

Philip ordered the duke of Parma, his commander in the Netherlands, to prepare his army to be shipped across the Channel in a fleet commanded by Admiral Marquis de Santa Cruz. England delivered one final insult in 1587 when Drake sailed into the Spanish port of Cadiz and destroyed 24 ships in an operation later called 'singeing the beard of the King of Spain'. Santa Cruz repaired the damage to his fleet, but died before the expedition was finally ready. His place was taken by the duke of Medina Sidonia. Word of the invasion electrified England and Elizabeth was compelled to raise a defence force of some 45,000 men from the local militia. A fleet commanded by Lord Howard of Effingham and Francis Drake gathered along the south coast of England.

The Spanish Armada set sail from Lisbon in spring 1588. The fleet comprised 130 vessels, including 20 great galleons. It was manned by 8,500 sailors and 19,000 soldiers; a further 27,000 troops - with 194 barges - were under orders to march from the Netherlands to Calais where they would combine forces. Elizabeth had heard reports of the great Spanish endeavour throughout the previous year but to keep an army waiting, ready for action, was enormously expensive; even the county militia had to be fed and equipped. The cost of sending troops to support the Dutch is estimated to have reached some £400,000 in the years from 1585-88. The expense of defeating an invasion force could use up the same amount in just one year: double the Queen's revenues. The treasury had already sold royal land to raise money.

All merchant shipping was taken over by

the Crown in the autumn of 1587 and local forces put on stand-by. However, local lords could not decide whether it was better to fight the Spanish on the beaches or concentrate further inland. Lord Burghley, who was in charge of funding the demands of army and navy, made his feelings clear: 'A man would wish, if peace cannot be had, that the enemy would not longer delay, but prove, as I trust, his evil fortune.' The English had one key advantage. English battle ship design had improved radically, creating ships with small turrets at either end and longer gundecks, making them faster and easier to manoeuvre. Above all, they could carry more and bigger guns. The first of these new form ships was the Dreadnought, launched in 1573, displacing 700 tons and carrying 31 tons of guns, almost five per cent of its overall weight. Between 1585 and 1604, Elizabeth spent over £1.5 million on her navy. The value of this investment was about to be tested.

In the middle of July, the Armada was sighted off Lizard Head on the southern tip of Cornwall. English naval forces mobilised, consisting of Lord Howards's fleet of 34 ships and Drake's fleet of 34 based in Plymouth, a London fleet of 30 ships and another fleet of 23 vessels off the Downs under Lord Seymour in the eastern English Channel. The first shots were fired outside Plymouth where the English fleet used their advantage in possessing more long-range cannons to sink one Spanish ship and damage several others. The duke of Medina Sidonia's instructions were not to engage the English navy, but to sail up the Channel, meet Parma's invasion fleet and escort him to England.

Towards the end of July, the Armada arrived at Calais, but Parma was not there. He was blockaded in Bruges by a Dutch fleet. The English fleet, now united, contented itself with long-range cannon fire, rather than risk close combat. The thousands of Spanish soldiers aboard Sidonia's ships never had the chance to board their enemies. At night, the English sacrificed eight of their

own ships by setting them on fire and letting them drift among the Armada. Sidonia cut his anchor cables and the Spanish fleet drifted northwards. The English harried them with broadsides, picking off individual ships. Unlike the English, who could replenish their ammunition supplies, the Spanish ran short and could not reply with the same intensity of fire. For the Spanish it was a terrible storm of gunfire. An officer on Sidonia's flagship reported '107 direct hits on the hull, masts and sails by cannon shot' and a veteran of the great victory over the Turks at Lepanto said he saw 'twenty times as much great shot.' Then the weather took over.

Strong winds prevented Sidonia from approaching either Dunkirk or Bruges to repair damage and re-supply. The Armada was driven into the North Sea. Sidonia had no choice but to sail around Britain, his crew suffering terrible hardships from hunger and thirst. Although realising the main danger had now passed, English ships managed to sink or capture 15 Spanish ships, while a fur-

ther 19 were wrecked on the Scottish and Irish coasts. Thousands of men died, under half of the original fleet limping back to Spain. It was not so much a victory for England as a catastrophe for Spain. One friar at El Escorial described it as 'the greatest disaster to strike Spain in over six hundred years,' while another said it was 'worthy to be wept over for ever...because it lost us the respect and good reputation that we used to have among warlike people.' The country went into mourning and the taxes raised to meet some of the enormous costs caused rioting. For England, having survived the onslaught of the greatest military power in the world, its reputation as a fighting nation rose higher, focusing even more attention on its navy which it would use in future centuries to establish its own global empire.

Massive Tudor cannon, nicknamed 'Queen Elizabeth's Pocket Pistol', now on view at Dover.

ROYALISTS AND ROUNDHEADS

The English Civil War was the culmination of centuries of strife between the king and the rest of society. Its result was to transform the nature of government in Britain.

The English Civil War of the 17th century was the last great civil war in Britain. The core of opposition to absolute royal power lay not just with aristocratic families but with the increasingly important middle classes. They had given strong support to the Protestant Reformation and grew intolerant of the autocratic King Charles I, whose court seemed suspiciously packed with Catholics. The English Civil War

Recreated musketeer pours a charge of gunpowder into his musket, prior to firing. After this, he would ram a musket ball into the barrel. [Philipp Elliot Wright/ English Heritage]

was to have a profound effect on the future government of Britain. It also brought about significant changes in the army, although past historians have tended to underrate its military importance. Hilaire Belloc commented,

'The numbers engaged upon either side of the struggle were usually small. Skirmishes outside country houses are dignified by the name of sieges; a mêlée of a few horse is often called a battle, while the lack of plan and purpose in much of the fighting makes the general observer underrate, if anything, the position of this English episode in the

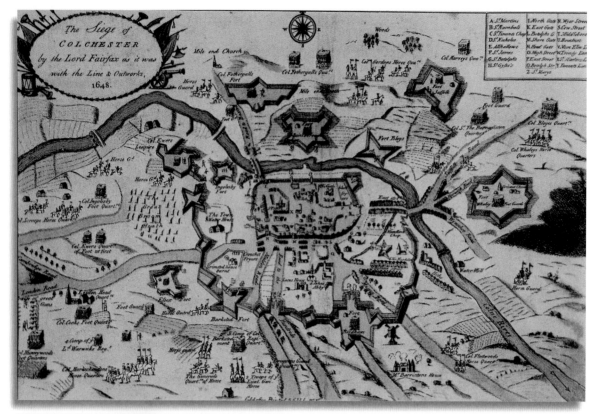

Contemporary map of the siege of Colchester in 1648 showing fortifications erected by the Parliamentarians as part of their siege of the city. Although the great battles of the period are best known, the majority of conflicts during the English Civil war took the form of sieges of important strategic centres. [Peter Newark's Military Pictures]

Engraved plate from a 17th century manual shows a musketeer using a powder horn to discharge the precise amount of gunpowder into the barrel of his musket. Military manuals introduced many European, especially Dutch, practices into British warfare, including the importance of drill, the Dutch being the most admired military nation at the time for their victorious war of independence against the Spanish.
[Peter Newark's Military Pictures]

general military history of the seventeenth century.'

Certainly, the numbers involved were small compared to the savage conflict in northern Europe known as the Thirty Years War, but its importance in British military history is enormous. At the beginning it was fought by civilian militiamen; by the end of it a regular, red-coated army had emerged, tactically a match for any in Europe. It would be the basis for the uniformed British Army of the 18th century. An entire military economy grew up on the back of it, supplying large quantities of equipment and weapons, which again would be the basis of Britain's arms industry in later centuries.

The son of James I of England (James VI of Scotland), Charles I represented a new Stuart dynasty that united the crowns of England and Scotland. Refusing to allow parliament to encroach on his authority, he ruled without one throughout the 1630s, but in 1639 resorted to arms against Scotland, although last minute negotiations prevented real fighting. A year later, he led a second army into Scotland and was beaten at the battle of Newburn. The costs of campaigning broke the royal finances. The king needed parliamentary revenue, but that was not forthcoming, even after Ireland was swept by bloody rebellion. The parliamentary leadership feared that a royal army would be used against them by a king determined on absolutist government. On 10 January 1642, Charles left for York to establish an independent military base. Parliament assumed control of government armed forces.

England was divided very evenly in 1642. A slight majority of the aristocracy supported Charles, while the merchant classes generally favoured Parliament. Most recruits for the King came from the north and west of England, while London, the south-east and Midlands provided the material and men for Parliament. However, there were few clear frontlines either politically, socially or geographically.

Charles could not compete with the wealth of London, but this did not prevent a bitter struggle between the two forces, the result of which could not be guessed at the outset. Indeed, in the first major battle of the Civil War at Edgehill in October 1642, the Royalist army had the best of the Parliamentarians, with Prince Rupert, Charles' 22-year-old nephew, leading a ferocious cavalry attack that forced Robert Devereux earl of Essex off the battlefield. Charles now moved his headquarters to Oxford and marched on London. Reinforced by London militiamen, Essex faced down the Royalists at Turnham Green and Charles, demonstrating fatal lack of nerve, retreated to Oxford.

With the support of Scotland, Parliament brought increased pressure to bear on Charles. In July 1644, the two armies met at Marston Moor and a Parliamentarian cavalry commander called Oliver Cromwell defeated Prince Rupert's cavalry, maintaining control of his horsemen to reinforce his own faltering footsoldiers to press for a victory. Charles, nevertheless, retained the support of southwestern England and Royalist Scots raised highland clans to temporarily re-establish Stuart authority in Scotland. A brief truce followed in which Cromwell urged a reform of Parliamentarian forces. Local militia units were replaced by a more professional trained army, paid for out of taxation, which became

CAVALIERS AND ROUNDHEADS

Popular fiction and Victorian paintings have given us very much the impression that the two sides in the English Civil War could be characterised as floppy hat-wearing, swashbuckling cavaliers on the one hand and helmet-clad, bible-clutching roundheads on the other, as though they wore different uniforms. In reality, the soldiers of both sides looked very similar. As campaigning took its toll on self-provided clothing, vast numbers of new clothes were ordered. The most popular colours for jackets and breeches of both sides were either red or blue as these were the cheapest to produce, involving a dyeing process of just one stage. Other colours could be achieved, but these involved two stages and more costly ingredients. Green, for example, could be achieved by dyeing first blue then yellow, while orange was first red and then yellow, purple being created from blue then red. A far cheaper alternative to using either red or blue dye was to use no dye at all but keep the natural colour of wool and both grey and bleached white were popular choices when a military budget

Recreated Civil War cavalryman. Beneath his breastplate he wears a buff coat made of ox hide which was strong enough to resist a sword stroke. [Philipp Elliot-Wright/English Heritage]

was tight. Large quantities of dyes were imported into Bristol from Amsterdam and the Caribbean, adding yet another reason for its capture as an important supply centre during the Civil War.

Armour largely survived in the form of breastplates and helmets and was worn by both pikemen and cavalry. Heavily armoured horsemen called cuirassiers wore full armour, but these were relatively rare on the battlefield and soldiers of both sides seem to have preferred to wear less armour rather than more, trusting to observation rather than blind defence. A more widely used form of armour was the buff coat, a sleeveless jacket with skirt made of thick ox hide which could resist sword strokes as well as long range shots.

Hats were of three main types and worn by both sides. The Monmouth cap and the montero were both made of knitted wool which was felted, the latter looking like a jockey cap with two brims at the front and back, its main purpose being comfort, keeping the head warm and dry. The more familiar broad brimmed felt hat, typical of the cavalier, was most likely worn by officers, as it was more expensive to produce, the most expensive version being made of beaver pelts imported from North America.

Musketeer of the recreated Fairfax Battalia. Gunpowder charges sufficient for one shot each are contained in the twelve wooden bottles called apostles that hang from the musketeer's bandolier. These were later superseded by charges wrapped in paper which proved more efficient as they created wadding which made the musket ball fit more tightly in the barrel. [Philipp Elliot-Wright/English Heritage]

Recreated pikeman of the English Civil War. He wears a breastplate with tassets to protect his thighs plus a helmet. Pikemen like this fought on both sides, but this particular re-enactor comes from the recreated Fairfax Battalia which would have fought on the Parliamentarian side. [Philipp Elliot-Wright/ English Heritage]

known as the New Model Army. It numbered some 22,000 men and consisted of twelve regiments of musketeers and pikemen, totalling 14,000, eleven regiments of cavalry and 1,000 dragoons, who functioned as mounted infantry. Fairfax succeeded Essex as captain general of the Parliamentarian army and Cromwell became lieutenant general. In June 1645, the two armies gathered for what would be the decisive battle of this first phase of the Civil War at Naseby.

The battlefield of Naseby is set among the rolling hills of Northamptonshire in the heart of England. The hills obscured the full strength of the opposing armies from each other. On the morning of 14 June, Prince Rupert rode out with a small force of Royalist cavalry to explore the area. He saw a group of Parliamentarian horsemen retreat which strengthened his confidence. He recommended that the King deploy his soldiers for battle. In reality, the troops Rupert had seen were merely scouts; behind the hills, Fairfax commanded an army 13,000 strong, 4,000 more than Charles had at his command. For once, Charles' timidity might have served him well by ordering a retreat, but Rupert was keen and the Royalist troops took to the field. A centre of some 4,000 footsoldiers armed with muskets and pikes was flanked by 5,000 cavalry. Fairfax arranged his men in a similar manner with cavalry on the flanks, the objective of both sides being to defeat one or other flank and thus roll up the centre, attacking the enemy on several sides. Fairfax ordered his dragoons to take position behind hedges on the left wing of the battlefield. He chose his ground well, for not only did he surprise the Royalists with the full strength of his army when he emerged over the ridge, he

compelled them to attack up the slope.

Prince Rupert got his blow in first. He led his veteran cavalry in an all-out charge uphill against the left wing of the New Model Army. The flanking fire of the dragoons failed to affect the outcome and the Parliamentarian cavalry was put to flight. However, the Royalists pursued them for miles, taking themselves out of the battle. In the centre too, the king's army had the upper hand, despite its inferior numbers. The New Model infantry regiments were driven back, but on their right flank, Oliver Cromwell had defeated the Royalist cavalry opposing his horsemen. His cavalry regiments did not gallop off in hot pursuit, but reformed and attacked the Royalist foot. Some surviving Parliamentarian cavalry from their defeated left also joined in, alongside Colonel Okey's dragoons.

Under attack from all sides, the king's infantry resisted to the last, a recently discovered trail of musket balls shows that the fighting continued for over two miles backwards. When Prince Rupert finally returned to the battlefield, over an hour after his victorious charge, it was to find the battle lost. Concentrations of musket balls located near Moot Hill mark where the veteran Royalist infantry made its last stand.

Naseby broke the military power of King Charles. Further minor combats confirmed his cause was finished and he surrendered himself to the Scots who sold him to Parliament for £400,000.

While the major battles are the most famous incidents of the wars, sieges were frequent too. Without command of the great cities of England, neither side could claim victory. Out of the 64 military engagements

Recreated musketeer blows on his matchcord to keep it alight so he can fire his musket. If not properly handled, lighted matchcords could prove dangerous by accidentally igniting nearby barrels of gunpowder. The musketeer's yellow jacket suggests he may be an Irish mercenary. [Philipp Elliot-Wright/English Heritage]

recorded in Joshua Sprigge's Anglia Rediva, an account of the New Model Army's achievements from 1645 to 1646, no less than 50 refer to towns and fortifications. Major sieges occurred at Portsmouth, York, Bristol and Gloucester. Many soldiers were busy defending or assaulting towns, which helps account for the small size of most field armies. Sieges were expensive too, involving the building of trenches and fortifications around a town and the use of artillery, especially mortars, to bombard it. At Newark, a 14 mile ring of earth ramparts was dug around the town, taking months to construct. Artillery, according to the Earl of Clarendon, was a 'sponge' which could never be 'satisifed'.

Usually, a town would surrender on seeing the arrival of artillery, having felt that it had already demonstrated its loyalty far enough. If a town waited for its walls to be stormed, it could expect little mercy from the soldiers forcing their way over the walls through a hail of fire. This was when the few major atrocities of the Civil War occurred. Bolton was stormed in May 1644 by Royalist forces who gave no quarter, slaughtering some 1,000 Parliamentarian troops alongside civilians. A contemporary account describes the Royalists,

'killing all before them without any respect, without the town by their Horsemen pursuing the poore amazed people, killing stripping and spoiling all they could meet with, nothing regarding the doleful cries of women or children.'

The earl of Derby was later held responsible for this war crime and executed.

In the two years following Naseby, the forces of Parliament were divided as various factions tried to gain control. Parliament voted that the army be disbanded but Cromwell took over its command and occupied London. The King escaped to the Isle of Wight and concluded an alliance with the Scots. In 1648, civil war broke out again. 'The story of the Second Civil War is short and simple,' wrote Winston Churchill in his History of the English Speaking Peoples. 'King, Lords and Commons, landlords and merchants, the City and the countryside, bishops and presbyters, the Scottish army, the Welsh people, and the English Fleet, all now turned against the New Model Army. The Army beat the lot.'

Cromwell, now acting as virtual military dictator, defeated the Scots at the battle of Preston. King Charles was recaptured and on January 30th 1649 was executed at Whitehall in London. Monarchy was abolished and Cromwell established a republic under military rule which lasted until 1660. Rebellions in Ireland and Scotland were crushed. Even the Dutch were beaten in a naval war. Cromwell had created a ferociously efficient and successful military machine.

Standardisation of equipment, clothing and weapons was introduced when Cromwell established the New Model Army in 1645. Set patterns were required from

Pikemen charge into combat from the recreated Fairfax Battalia, fighting on the side of the Parliamentarians. They wear red and blue clothes, but this is not a uniform, both sides wearing similar clothes because red and blue were simply the cheapest dyes available for military clothing. [Peter Newark's Military Pictures]

EXPERIMENTING WITH WEAPONS

Although pike and shot were dominant in the 17th century, experiments were made with other combinations of weapons. In the years before the English Civil War, the London Trained Bands were active in this field of research, having both the money and access to military manuals that encouraged free thinking on the subject. One path of research was inspired by classical sources. If tight formations of pikemen resembled the phalanxes of the ancient Greek world than perhaps the way of defeating them could be achieved through copying the Romans who ultimately triumphed over the Greeks. Thus, soldiers were armed with swords and shields and to a certain extent this proved successful in that the Spanish army employed numbers of 'sword and buckler' men. A variation on this was to make a pikeman look exactly like a Macedonian spearman by giving him a shield as well. Statues and prints of the period suggest that both combinations may well have been practised by London military enthusiasts.

Another avenue of exploration was to transform pikemen from a passive target to one which could achieve firepower as well. A typically English solution to this was to provide pikemen with bows. These pikemen could then soften up the enemy at a long range, until they came within range of musket fire, when the pikemen would then attach their bows to their pikes and protect the musketeers. A more up to date version of this was to fit the pikes with hooks half way down that could allow pikemen to rest light muskets or carbines on them and combine both forms of footsoldier. Alternatively, musketeers could be provided with sharp wooden stakes to create their own defence, an idea originally devised by the Swedish King Gustavus Adolphus. Another variant was to attach a pike head to the wooden rest used to support the musket. In the end, it was a little invention called the bayonet that truly transformed 17th century warfare and brought an end to pike and shot.

Royalist and Parliamentarian pikemen clash head-on in a recreated English Civil War battle. After the initial impact of lowered pikeheads, the combat would descend into a brutal scrum in which one side would hope to push the other backwards. [Military Illustrated]

Recreated unit of musketeers form a firing line before delivering a volley of shot. Most firefights were conducted at close range and were fought until one side had had enough and broke. The more popular knitted wool types of Civil War hat are worn by several of the soldiers. [Philipp Elliot-Wright/English Heritage]

manufacturers so that production quality could be checked at the Tower of London and standards maintained. Large quantities were ordered, creating a significant military industry in London and allowing for unit costs to be lowered. In one year, from 1645 to 1646, the following quantities were received: 8,050 matchlock muskets, 3,300 firelock muskets, 5,600 pikes, 10,200 coats, 9,000 shirts, 20,200 kitbags and 23,700 pairs of shoes. Many more contracts followed and London manufacturers must have grown rich on them, but it also ensured they delivered on time and quickly. The New Model Army had, for the first time seen in Britain, a uniform, consisting of a red coat and grey breeches with each

regiment bearing its own distinctive colour lining shown at the cuff.

Cromwell was quick to see the value of the new firelock musket. Its name is a little confusing for the firelock was different to the matchlock in that it did not require a burning cord to ignite the gunpowder inside the gun; it depended on a flint striking a metal plate to ignite the gunpowder. We now call it a flintlock. Initially, it was seen to be ideal for use by soldiers guarding artillery where a lighted cord could and did accidentally ignite barrels of gunpowder. The flintlock was much safer and though the lock was more intricate to produce, the fact that it did not need yards and yards of matchcord made it in the longer term cheaper. A 1,500 strong garrison at Lyme, for example, used five hundred-weight (254 kg) of matchcord every 24 hours. Also, the firelock gun was always ready to

Recreated demi-culverin explodes into action. Artillery was highly important during the English Civil War, both on the battlefield and in the numerous sieges that made up the bulk of combat during the war. [Philipp Elliot-Wright/English Heritage]

Contemporary map of the battle of Naseby, fought in June 1645 in Northamptonshire. King Charles I's army is shown at the top of the map while the Parliamentarian army under the command of Thomas Fairfax is shown at the bottom. The Parliamentarian baggage train to the bottom left proved a highly attractive target for the Royalist cavalry under Prince Rupert and by the time they returned to the main battlefield, the Royalists had lost their initial advantage.

fire whereas a matchlock first needed its cord lit and this was not always easy to do, particularly during a surprise attack. At the battle of Dunbar in 1650, Cromwell's dawn assault with firelocks caught most of the Scots soldiers with their matchcords unlit and only two regiments - those also armed with firelocks - were able to shoot back. Equally, the firelock was especially suitable for night raids, when a lit cord would give away the approach of troops. Thus, it became associated with more specialist troops and this probably gave it an elite appeal for ordinary soldiers.

Cromwell's enthusiasm for reform and innovation was applied also to the navy. A total of 207 new ships were added to the fleet and the Committee of Admirals improved both food and payment for sailors. The fruits of this were seen in the first naval clash between England and the Dutch in 1652. The Dutch were, of course, excellent seamen and expected no one to challenge their right to trade and sail where they pleased. Robert Blake, a commander of land forces during the Civil War, scored some remarkable successes against the Dutch fleet under Maarten Tromp, but at the battle of Beachy Head both sides suffered badly and Blake was seriously wounded. At the battle of Gabbard Bank in 1653, the English commander George Monck won another victory over the Dutch. A

blockade of Holland followed and Tromp led a major break-out but his fleet was savaged by the English ships and Tromp was killed in the action. England was now master of the North Sea.

The English Republic lasted until 1660 when monarchy was restored. Oliver Cromwell died in 1658 and in the power vacuum that followed, Monck supported Parliament in re-establishing civilian rule over military authority. This paved the way for the return of Charles II as king, with Monck as his captain general. The standing army was reduced to 5,000 men. A balance of power between monarchy, Parliament and the army seemed to have been found. In 1685, the consensus was rocked by the death of Charles II and the accession of his brother James II, a devout Catholic. His attempts to reassert Catholicism on an equal footing with the Church of England stimulated Protestant unrest which exploded at the battle of Sedgemoor in July of that year. The duke of Monmouth, the Protestant pretender to the throne, landed at Lyme but his small army was crushed; he was captured and beheaded.

James II's Catholic ambitions drove the political establishment to seek a replacement, especially after the suspiciously timely appearance of a male heir. The figure chosen was William of Orange, Stadtholder of the Netherlands and husband to James II's daughter, Mary. What followed was a combination of invasion and coup d'etat: William

Richly dressed and armoured ensign carries the colours of the recreated Fairfax battalia, a Parliamentarian unit. The red cross of St. George representing England is contained within a larger regimental emblem based on the personal insignia of the commanding colonel of the regiment. [Philipp Elliot-Wright/English Heritage]

landed with an army, James' generals betrayed him. James fled to France. In February 1689, William and Mary were crowned joint sovereigns. Later in the year, James II, with French support, landed in Ireland where his supporters led a revolt against William. In 1690, William crossed to Ireland and confronted James at the battle of the Boyne, one of the last battles in which two monarchs would face each other in a medieval-style contest for power. James failed to inspire his Irish troops to resist the English and Dutch and fled the field. Louis XIV of France denied James any further support for an invasion of England and a year later, with the battle of Aughrim and the loss of several key towns, James II's attempts at revolt were finished. A tragic byproduct of the war was the line of antagonism between Catholic southern Ireland and Protestant northern Ireland established for centuries to come.

During this period another revolution was taking place on the battlefield. The tactics of the pike and shot era were giving way to the bayonet and musket. With the introduction of the bayonet, the pikeman immediately became redundant. Every musketeer now became his own pikeman, able to protect himself from attack and lead a spirited charge. At first, the bayonet took the form of a dagger which was plugged into the end of the musket after firing had ceased. The battle of Killiecrankie, when English soldiers faced charging Highlanders, cruelly exposed the flaw in this invention. Unless the musketeers stopped firing early in the combat, the sword wielding Highlanders would be on them before they had time to fix their bayonets. Shortly afterwards, the socket

bayonet, which fitted over the end of the musket without preventing it from firing was introduced.

With the whole of an infantry regiment armed with flintlock muskets, a new discipline of firing was introduced. Volley firing had already been established by the Swedes and the Dutch and used during the English Civil War, but this was refined at the end of the 17th century by the introduction of firing by platoons in which smaller groups of soldiers fired in volleys creating a staggered, rippling effect up and down the main line, thus ensuring that all shots were not fired at once, leaving a vulnerable pause between loading, but still maintaining the impact of volleys on parts of the enemy line. The stage was now set for the red-coated British soldier in regimented lines to face the rest of the world and establish a legend of valour and victory.

GEORGIANS
AND JACOBITES

With the Act of Union in 1707, Georgian Britain was enormously confident and rich, but it faced a series of revolts by men and women loyal to the Stuart dynasty: the Jacobites.

Great Britain was born in 1707 with the Act of Union linking Scotland to England and Wales and creating 'one united kingdom'. A new flag fluttered above Britain's army: the Union Jack, or Union Flag, combining the English Cross of St. George with the Scottish Cross of St. Andrew and, later, the Irish Cross of St. Patrick. None of

Soldier of the Coldstream Regiment of Foot Guards kneels to fire his Short Land Pattern firelock musket. This superseded the Long Land Pattern musket in 1768 and by 1793 became the British Army's standard infantry weapon. Recreated by the Association of Crown Forces re-enactment group. [Peter Newark's Military Pictures]

Queen Anne's children survived, and political leaders in London feared the Scots might embrace her exiled Catholic half-brother James Edward Stuart. Instead, the newly united nation chose to invite a Protestant royal dynasty from Hanover to succeed Anne when she died.

King Louis XIV of France supported the exiled Stuart dynasty's claim to the British throne, partly out of sympathy for a fellow Catholic, but primarily to divert British resources in time of war. James II, his son, James Edward Stuart, and his grandson, Charles Edward Stuart ('Bonnie Prince

THE HIGHLANDERS

The popular view of these formidable warriors has been distorted by 18th century English prejudice and modern Scots nationalist propaganda. The conflict has been reduced to caricature, primitive Highlanders, wearing kilts and fighting with swords and shields, charge uniformed rows of English musketeers. A vision of barbarity or tragic romance, depending on your viewpoint. In reality, the Jacobite rebellions were civil wars in which Scots fought against Scots. Most Scots under arms fought for the government, not the Stuarts. Nor were the Highlanders dependent on primitive weapons. The Highland army which fought at Culloden in 1746 was equipped with muskets and bayonets. After the battle, only 190 broadswords were found on the field, as opposed to 2,320 muskets.

British recruiting officers knew a good fighter when they saw one and had already raised Highland units by the end of the 17th century. 'A Highlander would fight to the last drop of his blood at the command of his Chief,' wrote an impressed Major General David Stewart of Garth, 'and if he thought his honour or that of his clan insulted, he was equally ready to call for redress and to seek revenge.' The Independent Companies were not a great success to begin with, easily swung by clan prejudice or bribes and defrauding the British by charging for twice as many men as actually served. In 1715, they failed to quell the Jacobite rising, but by 1725, six new companies were raised from loyal clans, including three from the Campbells and one each from the Frasers, Grants and Munroes. A regimental order of 1725 indicates the uniform worn by these early Highland regiments:

'The officers commanding companies take care to provide a plaid clothing and bonnet in the Highland dress for the non-commissioned officers and soldiers, belonging to their companies, the plaid of each company to be as near as they can of the same sort of colour; that besides the plaid clothing, to be furnished each year, each soldier is to receive from his captain a pair of brogues every six weeks, a pair of stockings every three months, a shirt and cravat every six months.'

Highland clansmen of the middle of the 18th century are recreated here on Culloden Moor by the White Cockade Society, named in commemoration of the white rose worn in the hats of Jacobite supporters of Bonnie Prince Charlie. The central figure wears the original form of the Highland kilt, more a cloak that wraps around the entire body. Others are armed with the target and broadsword typical of Highland warriors. [White Cockade Society]

The plaid clothing worn by these soldiers was a traditional garment called a breacan-an-fheilidh, a combined cloak and kilt which was secured around the waist and looped over the shoulder, providing a blanket for sleeping in at night. The more familiar fheilidh-beg or little kilt was introduced later in the century. It seems likely that the predominant tartan worn was the Campbell pattern, consisting of dark blue and green stripes, and this evolved into the Government or Black Watch sett. Later, a red jacket would be added to the Highland costume, bringing the Scots warriors more into line with regular British troops. Before this, during the rebellion of 1745, loyal Highland soldiers wore a red cross on their bonnet. Weaponry included the traditional broadsword but not a shield and all Highland soldiers serving the Crown carried a musket and bayonet. Extra personal weaponry such as the dirk and two pistols could also be carried.

Caricature of ragged recruits outside an English pub in the late 18th century, who, once they join the army, will be transformed into the smart ram-rod straight soldier opposite them. Many recruits blamed the fact they were drunk for taking the King's Shilling to join the army. [Peter Newark's Military Pictures]

Charlie') were the focal points for opposition within Britain. Their supporters were known as 'Jacobites', Jacobus being the Latin version of James.

In 1708 James Edward Stuart landed in Scotland, a French expeditionary force pledged to follow him. But clan chiefs had little appetite for a Stuart rising and a storm scattered the French fleet. James returned to France and Louis XIV later recognised the Protestant succession in England as part of a Continental peace treaty. In 1715, John Erskine earl of Mar, raised an army of Jacobite Scots and clashed with loyal Scots under the command of Archibald Campbell duke of Argyll. The battle at Sheriffmuir was indecisive and the appearance of James Edward Stuart at Peterhead several weeks later could not compensate for Mar's failure. The rebellion fizzled out, James Edward fled back to France.

The Jacobite rising of 1745 was planned by the French in 1744 as a diversion. In 1743, King George II led a largely British army to victory over the French at Dettingen. In response, Louis XV raised an army of some 12,000 men with which to invade England. The chosen landing site was Maldon in Essex, from whence it would march on London and proclaim James VIII the new English king. Simultaneously a smaller force of 3,000 would sail to Scotland where it would be welcomed by Jacobite sympathisers. Charles Edward Stuart — Bonnie Prince Charlie — duly arrived in Paris to join the expeditionary force and in spring 1744 it began embarkation at Dunkirk. The French fleet sailed from Brest and encountered the British fleet off Dungeness. Battle was prevented by a gale that dispersed the ships. The storm also destroyed a number of French troop transports. The landing was cancelled.

Prince Charles Edward Stuart decided to go it alone. He received support from Irish shipowners whose usual trade of carrying slaves to the New World had been interrupted by the war with Britain. One of the Irish slaver's ships took Bonnie Prince Charlie to Scotland, loaded with 1,500 firelocks, 1,800 swords and £4,000 in gold, its owner hoping a successful outcome would allow him to return to his trade.

With a handful of companions, the Young Pretender landed on the shores of Loch nan Uamh, near Arisaig, in July 1745. Arriving without the thousands of French soldiers that the pro-Jacobite chieftains considered necessary for victory, he received a very muted welcome. Several chieftains refused to join him but, against his better judgement, Donald Cameron of Locheil lent his support and a Highland army of some 2,000 was raised.

Government forces in Scotland were commanded by General Sir John Cope and with a force of 3,000, mostly locally recruited, he decided to stand and fight at Prestonpans. The Jacobite army was commanded by Lord George Murray. John Home, a loyalist volunteer, describes the Jacobites' attack:

'The ground between the two armies was an extensive corn field, plain and level, without a bush or tree. Harvest was just got in, and the ground was covered with a thick stubble, which rustled under the feet of the Highlanders as they ran on, speaking and muttering in a manner that expressed and heightened their fierceness and rage.'

Units of dragoons on the wings of the British line lost their nerve and fled, exposing

the flanks of the British footsoldiers. Major Severne told the subsequent enquiry:

'A large body of their Left rush'd on obliquely on our Right Flank and broke the Foot as it were by Platoons, with so rapid a Motion, that the whole line was broken in a few minutes.'

It was an easy victory for the Jacobites. More men flocked to the prince's banner.

Charles Stuart sought to re-establish his dynasty: landing in Scotland was but a means to this end. However, he displayed little sense of urgency. Not until 31 October did the Jacobite army march on England. Carlisle's defences were virtually derelict and the city surrendered. The Jacobites marched on, took Manchester, and reached Derby on 4 December. They were within striking distance of London. However, to the prince's astonishment, Lord George Murray concluded it was time to retreat. The English army before them was over 14,000 strong. If they were surrounded, it would be a hanging party for the Jacobites. A record of Murray's advice survives:

'Lord George told him [the Prince] that it was the opinion of Every body present that the Scots had now done all that could be expected of them. That they had marched into the heart of England ready to join with any party that would declare for him, that none had, and that the counties through

Recreated 18th century military camp showing civilians dining with an officer. Armies were frequently accompanied by civilians, either the wives and dependants of soldiers, or official observers and guests of the officers. Accounts survive of civilian spectators treating a battle as an occasion for a picnic taken at a sufficiently safe distance from the combat. [Philipp Elliot-Wright/English Heritage]

MAKING THE RED-COAT

The red jacket of the British soldier in the 18th and 19th centuries is as synonymous with the British nation as the Union Jack and Rule Britannia. The choice of red for Britain's military uniforms has been linked with the red cross of St. George, the patron saint of England since the 14th century, but, in reality, its choice was purely practical and it could so easily have been blue. During the English Civil War, red and blue dyes were imported in large quantities to colour the clothes of both sides. Red and blue were the favoured colours, apart from various shades of grey from undyed wool, because they were cheap. They required only one stage in the dyeing process. Other colours, such as green or orange, required two stages of mixing colours and thus were more expensive.

Many Royalists favoured blue and when the monarchy was restored in 1660 several loyal units were clad in blue, no doubt in contrast to the red coats of Cromwell's New Model Army. Later, under William III, an early uniform code specified that 'all the Captains coats are to be of blue cloth faced with the same.' In 1702, however, faced with a major continental campaign, Marlborough, then supreme commander of British forces, wanted standardisation and rather than having both blue- and red-clad units, he decided 'officers be all clothed in red, plain and uniform, which is expected they shall wear on all marches and other duties as well as days of Review.' Thus, red became identified as the national military colour in contrast to the white of Bourbon France and later the blue of Revolutionary France.

The traditional process of dyeing uniforms red began with the cleaning of the fleece to make the cloth. This was steeped in human urine to remove any animal fat, urine being collected in large quantities from British pubs where it was kept in buckets for sale to the urine collector sometimes known as 'Piss Harry'. Once cleaned, the raw cloth would be taken to a dyeing house. A recipe for dyeing 60lbs of wool scarlet in 1823 lists the following ingredients: '1lb cochineal [powdered American insect], 3lbs madder, 6lbs argol [deposit from fermented wine], 3lbs alum [metal sulphate used as mordant to fix the colour], 4 pints tin liquor [derived from tin, a mordant used especially for creating scarlet], 6lbs cutbear [rock lichen found by the sea], and two buckets of urine.'

The alum, argol and tin liquor were boiled together in a vat for half an hour,

Recreated soldier of the 47th Regiment of Foot in full kit. These were the redcoats that fought around the world in Britain's first 'world war' against France, gaining an empire with territories in India and North America. In the 18th century, warfare in Britain became an activity conducted mainly abroad. [47th Regiment of Foot]

Rear of soldier of the 47th Regiment of Foot showing a folding canvas knapsack containing extra clothing and emblazoned with the Roman numerals of his regiment, as well as his black leather cartridge box. [47th Regiment of Foot]

then the madder and cochineal, the colouring, added for a further ten minutes. The wool was added and boiled for two hours in this liquid, which was then run off and the wool cleaned. A fresh liquid was made of 6lbs of cutbear and two buckets of urine and the wool steeped in this for a further two hours. Dyed and cleaned, scarlet cloth was stretched over tenter racks and left to dry outside. It was then combed with teasels, the bristly head of the Dipsacus plant, to create a nap, a soft fuzzy texture, on the cloth. Finally, tightly rolled, the cloth was immersed in hot water to give it a permanent lustre. British scarlet was now ready to be cut into the shapes required for stitching together into jackets.

One of the most famous areas of production for military cloth was Stroud in Gloucestershire where they graduated from producing Stroudwater scarlet to many other colours of cloth for uniforms around the world. An old Cotswold joke was that news of a rainy day in Moscow caused drunken celebration in Stroud, for it meant the pristine white uniforms of the Czar's soldiers would need to be replaced, guaranteeing weeks of extra work.

Close-up of typical Georgian military kit including a wooden canteen for water and a white linen haversack for carrying food and eating implements. [47th Regiment of Foot]

Close-up of musket lock showing the flint which, when triggered, would spark against the metal pan and thus ignite the gunpowder charge which fires the bullet along the barrel. [47th Regiment of Foot]

which the Army had pass'd had seemed much more enemies than friends to his cause, that their was no French landed in England, and that if there was any party in England for him, it was very odd that they had never so much as either sent him money or intelligence or the least advice what to do…'.

Murray recognised that the game was up. There was no serious support for the Stuarts in England. Bonnie Prince Charlie's dream was only a personal fantasy. The Prince was furious, but his followers started their long retreat.

William Augustus duke of Cumberland, and son of George II, was in command of the British Army. He had campaign experience on the Continent and led a highly professional army, day by day getting nearer to the retreating Jacobites. They marched to the sound of a song with music written by Purcell and with words that spoke of crushing the 'rebellious Scots' and 'God save our gracious King'; it was the first appearance of the British national anthem, the last verse tactfully removed in later, happier times.

Carlisle's Jacobite garrison surrendered and Bonnie Prince Charlie's army passed back over the frontier. Having been in the heart of England at the beginning of December, they were back on Scottish soil by the end of it. A small French force had landed on the east coast of Scotland in November and they, with Scots rebels, confronted a small army of loyalist Highlanders at Inverurie and won a neat little victory. This force now joined the main Jacobite army to lay siege to Stirling. The rebellion was turning into a Scottish civil war. Meanwhile, Cumberland was recalled south to face a possible French invasion. He was replaced by General Henry Hawley who recaptured Edinburgh, then marched on Stirling.

The two forces met at Falkirk on 17 January, clashing late in the afternoon during a storm. In the confusion, wind driving rain into the faces of the British regiments, many soldiers of both sides fled the field. 'The weather was so severe,' wrote a contemporary reporter, 'that he [Hawley] chose rather to abandon his camp, and retire to Linlithgow, than to destroy the Men by lying on their Arms all Night, wet to the skin, subject to continual Alarms.' On top of this, their ammunition was soaked. French and Jacobite troops occupied Falkirk, but neither side could truly claim a victory.

By the end of the month, Cumberland was back in Scotland and took a grip of the campaign. By April 1746 he had 9,000 regular troops, whereas Bonnie Prince Charlie's army had dwindled to some 5,000 men.

Lord George Murray persuaded the prince that a surprise attack at night might level the odds. But he overestimated the abilities of his troops. A night attack requires great discipline, and his men, inadequately supplied, were cold and hungry. Nevertheless, the prince's army headed north-eastwards across rough ground in pitch darkness to surprise the British troops at Nairn. Gaps soon appeared in the formation. The spirit among some of the Jacobites was good, they believed the British would be drunk, having celebrated Cumberland's birthday. Half way through the night, the army in a hopeless muddle, it was decided to abort the operation. The Jacobites returned wearily to their camp on Culloden, many falling immediately to the ground to sleep.

Contrary to the Jacobites' hopes, the

Recreated British soldiers of the late 18th century line up at Dover Castle.

British army toasted their commander's birthday with brandy, but then enjoyed a good night's sleep, rising at 4 A.M. to march on Inverness.

The Jacobites were organised into two lines with the majority in the front line, numbering some 3,800 troops, mainly Highlanders, including Camerons, Frasers, MacLeans, MacLachlans and MacDonalds. Two French regular units stood as reserves with a handful of cavalry while along the front of the army stood perhaps a dozen cannons. The British army had fifteen infantry battalions arranged in three lines, with substantially more cavalry in the form of three regiments, most of them on the left flank: a total of nearly 6,000 troops. Field guns were placed in the gaps between the battalions with the second line battalions covering the gaps between the first line battalions. At

about one o'clock firing began with the rebels firing their cannons. The British replied and the Jacobite units moved forward, impatient under fire and wanting to attack. Cannon fire was not very accurate at this time and many British shots are recorded as flying above the heads of the Jacobites, so it is likely that few casualties were caused by the British artillery.

Shouting requests to charge, after a quarter of an hour or so, the Jacobites were given the order to attack. According to one eye-witness

'They broke from the centre in three large bodies like wedges, and moved forward... and after firing very irregularly at a considerable distance, they rushed furiously in upon them [the British], thinking to carry all before them, as they had done on former occasions.'

The British artillery officers ordered a change of ammunition from cannon balls to canister which had the effect of a giant shotgun. The impact was murderous, killing dozens of men at close range, cutting down seveal clan chiefs, leading from the front. The charging units faltered, only to be met within seconds by the disciplined volleys of the British infantry. A British soldier remembered what happened next:

'When we saw them coming towards us in great Haste and Fury. We fired at about 50 Yards distance, which made hundreds Fall; notwithstanding which, they were so numerous, that they still advanced, and were almost upon us before we had loaded again. We immediately gave them another full fire.'

Then it was hand to hand with bayonets proving more than a match for swords and shields. Lieutenant-Colonel Robert Rich was caught in a ferocious fight to hang on to his regiment's colours, having a hand sliced off and several cuts to his head. 'Making a dreadful huzza and even crying 'Run, ye dogs!', they broke in between the grenadiers of Barrel and Monro [British battalions].' But as the Jacobites broke through the first line they were met by the fire and bayonets of the second British line.

A similar story was repeated along the line of battle. British soldiers fired regular volleys. The Jacobite left wing stopped on the boggy ground and never closed. The Jacobite right wing broke, running back over the moor. The British unleashed their cavalry. Bonnie Prince Charlie tried to rally these fleeing men, but his advisers, seeing the pursuing British cavalry, escorted him from the battlefield. His dream was over. The French reserve fired one volley at the advancing cavalry, then decided they too should leave the field. A general rout ensued and the British were merciless in pursuit. A British officer stated:

'The Rebels, besides their natural inclinations, had orders not to give quarter to our men. We had an opportunity of avenging ourselves for that and many other things, and indeed we did not neglect it, as few Highlanders were made prisoners as possible.'

In all, it is estimated that some 1,500 rebels were killed or wounded with perhaps 300 taken prisoner. The British lost 300 dead and wounded. After Culloden, Cumberland marched to Inverness, where he found a number of British prisoners who had been stripped of their clothes and thrust into a rat-infested dungeon. The British took great satisfaction in placing the rebels in the same cells. Cumberland was in no mood for compromise and issued a proclamation inviting all rebels to surrender. If they did, they would be treated leniently, which the majority were, but those that failed to give up their arms would be hunted down and executed.

A few rebel leaders clung to the belief of French intervention and two French frigates did sail into the Scottish lochs, but they were met by British sloops which gave them a hard battle and they then sailed away to France with some leading Jacobites on board. Pockets of resisting Jacobites were attacked by Cumberland who employed the Highland Independent companies against them. By July 1746, the rebellion was over and Cumberland returned to England. Bonnie Prince Charles, now spurned by most of his supporters for having brought this calamity on their land, fled before the avenging British and eventually set sail for France. It was the end of the last great military campaign on British soil.

FIX BAYONETS!

Despite the disappearance of the pike and the ascendancy of the musket, 18th century warfare still took place at close quarters. Lines of closely formed soldiers advanced to within firing range, less than a hundred yards, and then fire volleys until one side or the other decided it had had enough. Whole battalions could and did fire all their muskets at once in one deafening blast, but generally British soldiers were trained in platoon firing, that is smaller groups of soldiers firing one after the other, so that fire rippled up and down the line, allowing some soldiers to load while others fired, so a continuous fire could be maintained against an enemy. The average advancing rate of an infantry soldier of the time has been estimated at 70 paces per minute. This is also the effective range of the musket, so that a platoon could reckon on firing one volley and then perhaps another before the enemy made contact, unless of course it declined to make contact, preferring to engage in a firefight.

Against the Highland Jacobites, the situation was somewhat different. They preferred to charge over the intervening 70 paces, reducing their own casualties due to musket-fire and intimidating the waiting British. This method of warfare had already encouraged the development of the bayonet at the end of the 17th century, but not even platoon firing was enough to stem the fury of the Highland Charge in the middle of the 18th century. It was at Culloden that a breakthrough was made. Rather than ripple firing, the British let off great volleys of fire, once at long distance and then a second time at close-range. In the meantime, those soldiers in the front line did not bother to reload for the second volley but stood fast with their bayonets raised. This gave them the confidence to meet the Highland Charge when it closed. No British panicked at Culloden.

From this success came the germ of an idea that developed in the later 18th century. Against more traditional, less aggressive European armies, who preferred the firefight, a variation of the Highland tactics was devised. Rather than practising platoon firing, British soldiers simplified the situation by letting off massed volleys and then, holding their muskets and bayonets level with their waists, would charge the enemy. The bayonet had become an offensive weapon. To this was added the use of skirmishers who would advance ahead of the main formations firing at will at the enemy. Thus, weakened by skirmish fire and then two massed volleys, the enemy would be finally broken by a determined bayonet charge through the smoke of musketry. It was this simple tactic, refined during the Seven Years War and the wars in America, that would bring the British Army its famous victories against the armies of Napoleon.

Recreated British grenadier with a bearskin cap of the sort sent to North America to fight rebels during the American War of Independence. [Philipp Elliot-Wright/English Heritage]

REDCOATS AND NAPOLEON

With Napoleon across the Channel threatening invasion,
Britain transformed itself into a formidable military power,
creating new taxes to pay for the huge demand in troops and
the building of forts along its coast.

Public opinion in Britain showed initial sympathy with the French revolutionaries, praising their pursuit of freedom against the despotic Louis XVI. Three years into the revolution, however, the British began to see a different side to the turmoil in France. In September 1792, imprisoned priests and aristocrats were murdered, mob-

Two faces of Britain's armed forces that challenged Napoleon. On the left is a recreated Royal Marine who would have fought on board ship, while the land-based soldier on the right is of the recreated 42nd Royal Highland Regiment. The little cloth pouch on the Royal Marine's cross-straps contains spare flints for his Brown Bess musket. [John Norris]

rule triumphed over the ideals of revolution. A broad sheet declared:

'The French are at this Time the most distracted Nation under Heaven, and what is worse, they are the most wicked... teaching John Bull to eat Revolution-Soup, dished up with human Flesh and French Pot-Herbs? I love Liberty with Law, such as we have in England, as well as anybody does; but that Liberty without Law, which makes Men eat one another, can come only from the Devil, who would eat us all.'

This melodramatic portrayal of events in France encapsulated a truth which the British

Martello tower at Dymchurch. These round towers were built at strategic locations along the British coast against French invasion.

knew well; liberty without the rule of law means nothing.

Britain declined to join other European countries in an armed assault upon Revolutionary France in 1792. But the execution of the French king in 1793 led the British to expel the French ambassador. France declared war on Britain. At Toulon, the British endeavoured to destroy the French fleet, but French soldiers recaptured the forts commanding the harbour and forced the British to retreat. One of the French officers involved was a young lieutenant called Napoleon Bonaparte, who was rapidly promoted. Catapulted to command an invasion of northern Italy, he defeated the Austrian army and by 1798 was in charge of an army earmarked for the invasion of Britain.

By employing mass conscription the revolutionary authorities assembled very large armies. Britain turned to its traditional system of local defence. The militia had already been improved in 1757 when Parliament ordered every English and Welsh county to recruit a set number of men and pay for their military service out of local taxation. This was to raise some 32,000 men who would be trained for one full month every year. In practice, most men with money could avoid service with the militia and there were not enough others available to meet the targets set. The Supplementary Militia Act was passed in 1796, requiring a further 60,000 militiamen from England, another 4,400 from Wales and, for the first time, 6,000 men from Scotland. Allowances were made for the larger population size of industrialised areas, as opposed to rural regions, and cities provided several battalions, while country parishes provided smaller units. Gentlemen were also

encouraged to set up their own, privately-funded regiments and local professionals, shopkeepers and farmers volunteered for home defence service separate from the militia. Because the government paid nothing towards these forces, they could equip themselves as they wished and frequently chose elaborate, attractive uniforms. A private's uniform in the fashionable London volunteer corps could cost up to £50.

Regular militiamen were enlisted for five years and were placed continuously under arms, garrisoned away from their home regions so that if they were called on to quell civil disturbances they could do so without any conflict of loyalty. Although a form of conscription, there were many exemptions, including those who were members of other volunteer corps, apprentices, dissenters, and poor men with one legitimate child. Wealthy men who preferred not to be in the local militia could pay a fine of £20 or find a substitute to serve in their place.

The demand for substitutes led to competition in which local parishes ended up paying a higher bounty for the recruitment of militiamen than the army and this drained good men away from regular service. One Rochdale man put himself up for sale, demanding a guinea for every inch of his 63 inch height, almost ten times the regular army bounty of £7/12/6d. He received it, and another man sold himself, like butcher's meat, at so much per pound. By 1807, out of 26,085 men enlisted in England, only 3,129 were those who had been called first, the rest being substitutes.

In 1799 the government passed an Act which provided that while militiamen were guaranteed not to be sent to the disease-rid-

TESTING SHARPE'S RIFLE

Richard Sharpe, the fictional character created by best-selling author Bernard Cornwell, is a rifleman in the Peninsular War, a green-jacketed soldier who fights not in the traditional style of redcoats lined up in close-order with muskets, but in a newer, more contemporary form of warfare, performing as an individual on the battlefield with a high-performance weapon. Regiments of riflemen were a relatively new concept in the Napoleonic Wars, derived from the riflemen recruited during Britain's wars in North America in the middle of the 18th century when the value of a looser form of battlefield tactic became apparent. Soldiers armed with rifles and wearing virtual camouflage clothing now skirmished in front of the main lines of redcoats, crouching out of sight and taking pot-shots at the opposition before the main firefight started.

The weapon that made this new form of warfare possible, used by Sharpe in fiction and the 95th Rifles in reality, was the Baker Rifle. Like all rifles, it derived its name from the rifled barrel that improved the accuracy of fire in comparison to the older smoothbore musket. There is much mythology associated with this weapon, however, particularly from British sources and tests with both muskets and rifles show that although the musket is less accurate, it is faster to load and perhaps explains why the French never adopted the rifle in the way the British did, happy to use skirmishers armed with muskets who were equally successful if not more so than British riflemen in battlefield confrontations. The French substituted quantity for quality, preferring a higher number of weapons. Other factors also hampered the performance of the Baker Rifle, such as the early issuing of bullets intended for cavalry carbines that were slightly too large for the rifle barrel and so needed a mallet to tap the ramrod as the bullet was pushed into the gun. This deformed the bullet and made it inaccurate in flight, thus reducing the original advantage of the rifled barrel.

That said, the results that could be achieved with a Baker Rifle were impressive. Tests showed it could regularly hit a target at some 200 yards distance. The India Pattern musket in comparison had a range of 300 yards but hit home with only 50 per cent of shots at 100 yards. Some remarkable feats of accuracy were achieved with the Baker Rifle, such as that by Tom Plunkett of the 95th Rifles at Cacabelos in 1809. Spurred by a bet, Plunkett lay on his back with his rifle supported on his crossed legs and aimed at the French General Colbert who was on the other side of the river Cua. A shot rang out and Plunkett's bullet struck the General in the forehead at a range of 300 yards. Plunkett followed this up by picking off the General's trumpeter as well.

SURRY YEOMANRY.

Surrey Yeomanry cavalryman painted by Thomas Rowlandson for a print published in 1798. Such soldiers were volunteers who were usually gentlemen of some means who could equip and uniform themselves at their own expense. They were raised specifically in the 1790s to counter the threat of invasion by Napoleon and supplemented the Militia. [Peter Newark's Military Pictures]

Southwark Volunteer painted by Thomas Rowlandson for a print published in 1798. Several Acts in the 1790s raised a substantial body of Volunteer soldiers to act as a Home Guard force in case Napoleon invaded Britain. If they served away from home, these soldiers would be paid, which tended to cream off the best young men from the Militia until later legislation merged the two organisations. [Peter Newark's Military Pictures]

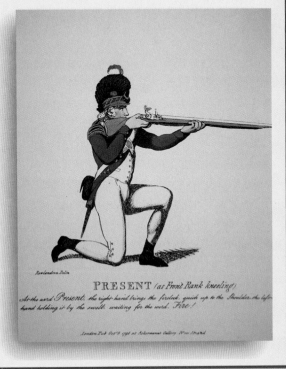

PRESENT *(as Front Rank kneeling)*

Battle off Cape St. Vincent in which the Royal Navy defeated a Spanish fleet in 1797, thus preventing them from joining forces with the French Navy. Such victorious actions reinforced the fact to Napoleon that no invasion could take place without mastery of the sea and the Royal Navy could not be mastered. [Peter Newark's Military Pictures]

den West Indies, they could be called upon to serve in Europe. Some 10,000 militiamen were shipped to the Netherlands. William Surtees, a volunteer from Northumberland, thought the transition from home to abroad was too quick:

'Nothing could exceed the materials of which these two battalions were composed, had they the advantage of a little more experience; and no troops could fight better than they did, after gaining the support and countenance of the old regiments which were sent to reinforce them. But I confess with shame, we showed a great want of nerve in the early part of the day... everyone seemed intent only on making the best of his way to the rear.'

Between 1805 and 1815, some 100,000 militiamen joined the regular army for service abroad. Some militia officers objected to this process, declaring that foreign service took the best local men, leaving only 'refuse' to serve at home. There was even competition among regular regiments for who could recruit the best militiamen. George Napier of the 52nd, recruiting in Limerick, was approached by

'ten very handsome militia soldiers, six feet high, who said they would volunteer with whichever officer of the line could beat them in running and jumping. Of course, in order to get these fine fellows, we all tried and exerted ourselves to the utmost.. we had a hard struggle with Pat; but I was beat by them.'

Fortunately, another officer proved more athletic and the Irish militiamen joined his regiment. By 1805, the strength of the militia inside Britain was as high as 89,809 men, although the total number, including part-time soldiers, private units, and those willing to fight if necessary, has been estimated at half a million, based on replies to a govern-ment census of the period. The regular British Army had also grown, from 40,000 men in 1789 to 250,000 in 1814.

Ireland was the weakest point in Britain's defences. A French naval force set sail from Brest in December 1796 with 43 warships and transport ships bearing 13,000 troops. The invasion intended to capitalise on an uprising against British rule that began in 1795. However, the invasion fleet was scat-tered by strong winds. Part of it arrived in Bantry Bay, but high seas prevented a landing and the French Admiral de Galles abandoned the project. Five ships were lost in the storms and a further six were captured by the British fleet.

In 1797, a small expeditionary force got closer to Britain by landing in Wales. This group of some 1,200 French soldiers was led by William Tate, an adventurer from South Carolina who had fought with the colonists against Britain in the American Revolution. Now a colonel in the French Army, he landed at Fishguard in Pembrokeshire. A week previ-ously, a smuggling ship had been wrecked off the Welsh coast and every cottage nearby had its own cask of wine. This was the undo-ing of the French troops. One eye-witness declared that

'Gluttony was followed by intoxication,

and here the finger of heaven was manifestly visible... the intemperate use of [the wine] produced a frenzy that raised the men above the control of discipline, and sunk many of their officers below the power of command; and to this principally, in gratitude to the Divine Being, may be ascribed the so speedy and happy termination of a business that seemed to menace a much more distressing catastrophe.'

Meanwhile, a hastily assembled British force under Lord Cawdor was marching to the rescue. He assembled 120 Cardiganshire Militia, 120 Pembroke Fencibles, 50 Castlemartin Yeomanry Cavalry, and 150 sailors from Milford. Discipline was proving a severe problem in the French force, as one incident revealed. A Welsh farmer named Thomas had his silver watch, silver shoe buckles, and some money stolen by some Frenchmen. He complained to Tate, who ordered that the soldier responsible should be executed. His fellow soldiers refused to shoot him and when French officers volun-teered to carry out the order, the soldiers declared they would shoot the officers instead. Tate decided it would be best to sur-render, the final decision to capitulate apparently influenced by the presence of sev-eral hundred Welsh women clad in traditional red cloaks and black felt hats with the British force. Reports spoke of several thousand red-clad troops of the line, convinc-ing Tate he faced a regular army. Thus, the last military force to invade Britain surren-dered to a British home defence unit half its size.

The republican French created the 'Army of England' at Dunkirk, but the invasion was postponed after the defeat of their Spanish allies at Cape St Vincent. The Army of England remained to menace Britain while Napoleon sailed for Egypt. In August 1798, another assault was made on Ireland with 1,200 French troops landing at Killala Bay, but these were surrounded by Lord Charles Cornwallis and forced to surrender. A reinforcing French fleet was destroyed at sea by Sir John Warren.

The threat of an invasion recurred in 1804. 'The Channel is but a ditch and anyone can cross it who has the courage,' declared Napoleon, now dictator of France. 'Let us be masters of the Straits for six hours and we shall be masters of the world.' He gathered 130,000 troops at Calais and a fleet of over 2,200 barges, fishing boats and other potential landing craft. He had a medal struck in order to reward his victorious troops for conquering England. The British navy and militia were ready to face the invasion, but the British government thought an additional line of defence was needed. In 1803, a military engineer, Captain William Ford proposed that a chain of towers be built on the most likely invasion beaches. Each tower would mount a single gun that could offer crossfire to the landing troops. The inspiration for this came from a round fortified tower in, ironically, Napoleon's birthplace of Corsica at Mortella Point which had in 1794 defied a British naval assault for two days.

The government authorised construction of a defensive line across southern England. The first element was a canal or ditch stretching 23 miles from Pett Level to Hythe. Work began in the autumn of 1804 and only after some £200,000 had been spent did people start questioning whether a 30 foot wide

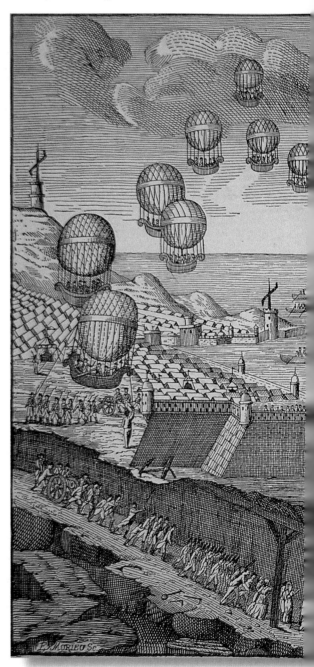

French print of 1803 showing how Napoleon's army might invade Britain, using a tunnel beneath the Channel, an armada of troop ships and balloons armed with soldiers. Continued threats of invasion encouraged an enormous expenditure on coastal defences and the raising of militia units, resulting in the creation of new taxes to fund it, such as income tax, first introduced in 1798. [Peter Newark's Military Pictures]

ditch would really stop an army that had just crossed the Channel. A plan to flood Romney Marsh was rejected before work began. The towers seemed much more practical and work started in the spring of 1805 under the direction of the Board of Ordnance and Royal Engineers. It was an enormous undertaking, each tower requiring at least half a million bricks. The main building contractor, William Hobson, was suspected of making a fortune out of the 103 towers which eventually lined the coast from Newhaven in Sussex to Aldeburgh in Suffolk. Each cost £3,000. An additional two redoubt forts were built at

Green-coated riflemen were the elite of the British army during the Napoleonic wars, selected for their intelligence and expected to perform independently, more like a modern soldier rather than part of a regimented firing line. These riflemen were the inspiration behind the fictional character of Sharpe invented by best-selling author Bernard Cornwell. [95th Rifles Regiment of Foot Living History]

Dymchurch and Eastbourne as supply and command centres.

Called Martello towers after the original inspiration of the fort at Mortella Point in Corsica, they all took the same form: round tapering towers 30 feet tall with an outer wall facing the sea some 13 feet thick. They had three floors with the entrance on the first floor reached only by a ladder which could be pulled inside during a siege. Some were surrounded by a dry moat. The first floor had living quarters for a garrison of some 24 men and an officer, while the ground floor was used to store ammunition. The top floor was the gun platform with a two and half ton cannon mounted on a central pivot which allowed it to be pointed in any direction. It could fire a 24lb shot a mile out to sea. On flat open beaches, they were positioned 600 yards apart from each other allowing at least 15 towers to direct fire on an approaching fleet. They were manned by the Royal Artillery who were supported by Artillery Volunteers from the local communities.

They were never used. In 1805 Nelson defeated a French-Spanish navy at Trafalgar and Napoleon accepted that there was little chance of a successful invasion. Work on the towers nevertheless continued until 1812. In later years, the Martello towers were used by the Coastguard to thwart smuggler gangs. Today, there are 43 Martello towers left and some have been restored and are open to the public, such as the Wish Tower at Eastbourne.

From 1808 Britain took the war to the enemy with increasing success. Home interest in the Peninsular War was considerable and a whole host of memoirs by soldiers who fought in the campaigns became best-sellers among a readership keen to hear about war abroad against Napoleon's armies. Two of these memoirs, Twenty Five Years in the Rifle Brigade by William Surtees and Adventures in the Rifle Brigade by Captain John Kincaid, concentrated on the experiences of soldiers in the green-jacketed 95th Rifles. Fiction in the early 19th century was also affected by the war. Soldiers and espe-

cially officers featured heroically in numerous romantic novels. In Pride and Prejudice, written in 1813, Jane Austen describes the effect officers could have on young ladies:

'Their eyes were immediately wandering up in the street in quest of the officers, and nothing less than a very smart bonnet indeed, or a really new muslin in a shop window, could recall them.'

Later, when a handsome young man is spotted, his flaw is obvious:

'His appearance was greatly in his favour; he had all the best part of beauty, a fine countenance, a good figure, and very pleasing address.. the young man wanted only regimentals [a uniform] to make him completely charming.'

British riflemen of the recreated 95th Rifles Regiment of Foot. Armed with the Baker Rifle, these soldiers functioned as skirmishers, working together in pairs, one loading while the other fired. [95th Rifles Regiment of Foot Living History]

SOLDIERS IN RAGS

Although the glamour of wearing a uniform was what attracted many young men to joining the army, this smartness rarely lasted beyond the first few weeks of a campaign. In Portugal and Spain, the extreme temperatures and rough terrain quickly reduced uniforms to rags. George Wood of the 82nd recalls his appearance on campaign: 'Our coats were patched over with different colour cloth... my own coat was mended with the breeches of a dead Frenchman, which I found on the field - the only trophy I yet had to boast of having retained from the spoils of the enemy.' John Patterson of the 50th had an even harder time: 'Our clothes were worn to rags, the jacket being no better than 'a thing of shreds and patches', metamorphosed from red to a sort of muddy claret colour; the other garments were... pieced in a manner that would have qualified the wearer to perform the part of Harlequin. The whole attire was surmounted by a nondescript article, vulgarly called a cocked hat, which... formed a good reservoir for rain, its angular point answering the purpose of a waterspout, while the flap hanging over the dorsal region, like that of a London coal

heaver, imparted to the owner, a look of most dubious character.'

Wellington, British commander during the Peninsular War, famously cared little about the detail of uniforms. 'He never harassed us with reviews, or petty annoy-

Soldiers of the recreated 42nd Royal Highland Regiment march through a Belgian village at Waterloo to commemorate the great victory won there by the British and their allies in 1815. This final triumph over Napoleon was the high point of the British army of the Georgian period and gave its name to buildings and places throughout Britain. [Peter Newark's Military Pictures]

ances,' recalled William Grattan, 'which so far from promoting discipline, or doing good in any way, have a contrary effect... Providing we brought our men into the field well appointed, and with sixty rounds of good ammunition each, he never looked to see whether their trousers were black, blue or grey; and as to ourselves (the officers), we might be rigged out in all the colours of the rainbow if we fancied it. The consequence was, that scarcely any two officers were dressed alike! Some with grey braided coats, others with brown; some again liked blue; while many from choice, or perhaps necessity, stuck to the 'old red rag'.' So much for the idea of uniformity, promoted in later years by toy soldier manufacturers in which every soldier looked alike, down to his last brass button.

Caricature attacking the work of a Royal navy press gang in 1794, forcing civilians to serve on board ship. In reality, such recruiting methods were usually aimed at returning seamen and rarely included land-based civilians with no experience of the sea. [Peter Newark's Military Pictures]

THE OLD SAUCY

SEVENTH,

Or Queen's Own Regt. of

Lt. Dragoons.

COMMANDED BY THAT GALLANT AND WELL KNOWN HERO,

Lieut. General

HENRY LORD PAGET.

YOUNG Fellows whose hearts beat high to tread the paths of Glory, could not have a better opportunity than now offers. Come forward then, and Enrol yourselves in a Regiment that stands unrivalled, and where the kind treatment, the Men ever experienced is well known throughout the whole Kingdom.

Each Young Hero on being approved, will receive the largest Bounty allowed by Government.

A few smart Young Lads, will be taken at Sixteen Years of Age, 5 Feet 2 Inches, but they must be active, and well limbed. Apply to SERJEANT HOOPER, at

N. B. This Regiment is mounted on Blood Horses, and being lately returned from SPAIN, and the Horses Young, the Men will not be allowed to HUNT during the next Season, more than once a week.

BOOTH AND WRIGHT PRINTERS, NORWICH.

Recruiting poster for the 'Saucy 7th', the Queen's Own Regiment of Light Dragoons, of around 1810. This was a unit of the regular army and was regarded as highly glamorous, although a note at the bottom of the poster warns soldiers they will not be able to hunt more than once a week. [Peter Newark's Military Pictures]

Soldiering had become sexy. The military represented the very best of manhood in the eyes of a British home audience no longer personally exposed to the reality of war.

Many who joined the army then, as now, were in their late teens. William Lawrence, also from Dorset, became a building apprentice at the age of 14, but after being beaten by his master, ran away a year later to Poole. In Dorchester, he saw some soldiers.

'I said I wanted to be a soldier too. The ostler knew where he could enlist me and took me straight to the rendezvous which was a public-house. Inside was a sergeant of artillery, who gave him [the ostler] two guineas for bringing me and myself five for coming. My measurements were taken - which caused a lot of amusement - and I was put into an old soldier's coat. With three or four yards of ribbon hanging from my cap, I paraded around town with the other recruits, entering almost every public-house, treating someone or other.'

Unfortunately, several farming friends of his father saw Lawrence and though he offered them ale to say nothing, his father found him and took him before a magistrate who said he had a choice of going back to his apprenticeship or facing prison.

On his way back to his apprentice master, Lawrence made another break for it. He fell in with another soldier, but had to admit he was an apprentice. The soldier then hid him at his home and took him secretly to the barracks of the 40th Regiment of Foot. The colonel asked him what trade he was in.

''I'm a labourer,' I replied. 'Labourers make the best soldiers,' he said and offered me a bounty of two and half guineas, which was considerably less than the sixteen we had been expecting so we decided to try the Marines. Their recruiting sergeant promised us 16 guineas bounty when I arrived at their Plymouth headquarters but this did not suit my conductor because, after paying the coach expenses, there would have been nothing left over for him.'

He decided to go back to the 40th Regiment and enlisted.

'Next day I received my clothes, and about a week later was sworn in before the magistrate, receiving my bounty at the same time [two pounds twelve shillings and sixpence]. I was very mistaken about the money lasting.'

Ordinary sailor painted by Thomas Rowlandson for a print published in 1799. Usually regarded as the lowest of the low, British sailors and the Royal Navy enjoyed a huge rise in their popularity and respect from the British public following their series of victories over Napoleon's navy, culminating in the battle of Trafalgar. [Peter Newark's Military Pictures]

Leaving barracks in Taunton, Somerset, Lawrence marched with his comrades to Winchester.

'There we remained for about a month. I had begun to drill twice a day. I soon learnt the foot drill and was then put on musketry drill. After Winchester, we moved to Portsmouth. We were there a week before being ordered in to barracks at Bexhill in Sussex. Our 1st battalion was there and in order to make it 1,000 strong, a number of men were drafted into it from our battalion - the 2nd. I was one of them. Soon orders came for us to go to Portsmouth; we were about to embark on foreign service.'

Only six women were allowed to travel with a company of 100 men and Lawrence noted the tearful farewells as soldiers said good-bye to their wives, children and lovers on the morning of departure. 'As my family did not have the slightest idea where I was,' remembered Lawrence, 'there was no one to throw so much as a parting glance at me.' The year was 1806 and Lawrence was just 16.

He set sail for South America where his battalion fought against Spanish commercial interests and in 1808 with the beginning of the Peninsular War he

found himself in Portugal. He survived some of the toughest battles of the Peninsular War, including Badajoz and Vitoria. He was wounded and promoted, eventually becoming a sergeant. He is even present at Waterloo in 1815. It was a remarkable career, particularly when one considers the very high casualty rate during the Peninsular War, with most wounded soldiers not recovering. Charles O'Neil of the 28th (North Gloucestershire) Regiment put it bluntly

'Our whole regiment was called, and every man examined... We were one thousand strong, when we commenced our Peninsular campaign. Only seven men, with our colonel, who had lost one arm, were now alive! Nine hundred and ninety-two had fallen upon the field of mortal strife, and only seven men, beside myself, could be found, in less than one year after the bloody battle of Waterloo!'

Lawrence had been lucky indeed and concluded his working life running a pub with his wife in Dorset. When his wife died, he 'wrote to the authorities at Chelsea and, through the influence of a kind gentlemen, I obtained an additional threepence a day on my pension, making a shilling in all.' Lawrence died in 1869. By then, Britain's armies were engaged in a different kind of warfare in which they defended the interests and honour of an empire that stretched all around the world.

Martello tower built on the coast of Guernsey to protect it from the threat of invasion from Napoleon's army. Now open to the public, it is surrounded by specially cast cannon and recreated figures representing the original militia soldiers that manned it, including the Captain of Rousse tower inspecting his command. [Peter Newark's Military Pictures]

VICTORIANS AND EMPIRE

*The British Empire continued to expand during
the nineteenth century, but the military resources
to protect these new territories were kept to a minimum.*

Between the defeat of Napoleon in 1815 and the beginning of the First World War in 1914, Britain enjoyed an unprecedented period of peace and prosperity. There were no foreign invasions, no civil wars, no rebellions. All eyes, instead, were directed abroad as the British army and navy protected the interests of British trade and government around the world. There were a myriad of wars and battles fought in exotic locations from Burma to New Zealand, from Canada to South Africa, all of them reported in the form of articles with wood engraving illustrations printed in newspapers such as The Times and The Illustrated London News. Britons became proud of their Empire and the soldiers and sailors that defended it. First-hand accounts of campaigns against Zulus and Fuzzy-Wuzzies vied with fictional adventures set in India or Africa, all project-

HMS Warrior, now moored and open to the public at Portsmouth, was a revolutionary armoured ship. Not only was it steam-powered, but its guns, engine and boiler rooms were encased in an armoured box. Built of wrought iron plates bolted to 18 inches of solid teak, it could stand up to any gun fire and was the largest, fastest and most powerful warship in the world when launched in 1861. [Peter Newark's Military Pictures]

ing an image of sturdy white men up against the forces of darkness that encouraged the British to see themselves as superior in many ways to the people and civilisations of other countries. To be born British at this time, to paraphrase Cecil Rhodes, was to win first prize in the lottery of life. This was not to say, however, that there were no conflicts at all at home.

One of the major roles of the British army garrisoned at home was to be ready to quell civil disturbances. There were no significant civil police forces in Britain in the 18th and early 19th centuries and so if people and property were to be protected from rioters and protesters then local government called upon the militia or regular troops. The duty of the army was to be loyal to the Crown and

the government and maintain law and order. For this reason, soldiers recruited in one region would frequently be garrisoned in another area so local ties would not affect their ability to perform this role. Throughout this period there were numerous violent protests, ranging from the anti-industrial Luddites who smashed factory machinery to the Chartists who agitated for electoral

Battery of artillery firing a salute at the Tower of London on Queen Victoria's Birthday in 1897. Tower Bridge can be seen in the background. This year was also her Diamond Jubilee and was cause for enormous celebration, with soldiers coming from all across the Empire to parade in her honour. [Peter Newark's Military Pictures]

Recruiting Sergeant-Major Johnstone of the Cavalry depot inspects an aspiring cavalryman. The original caption to this photograph, taken around 1895, reads: 'Raw material and the finished article', making clear the transformation the army can make to a young man. [Peter Newark's Military Pictures]

reform. The most bloody disturbance occurred in London in 1780 during the anti-Catholic Gordon riots which lasted a week and in which 285 people were killed by regular troops. One of the latest incidents occurred in 1893 when two striking miners were killed by soldiers at Featherstone in the West Riding. Perhaps the most notorious clash of soldiers and civilians in Britain was at Peterloo in 1819.

The name Peterloo was in fact a satirical reference to the use of military force to disperse a political meeting that took place in St. Peter's Field in Manchester; the pride of Waterloo giving way to the shame of Peterloo was how the newspapers of the time portrayed it. The incident began with the gathering of some 60,000 people to hear the radical politician Henry Hunt talk about parliamentary reform and the repeal of the protectionist Corn Laws which had sent bread prices soaring. The organisation of the protesters was carried out with military precision and symbolism and it may be this that sparked concern among the local magistrates. Samuel Bamford, one of the organisers, described their appearance: 'Every hundred men had a leader, who was distinguished by a sprig of laurel in his hat; others similarly distinguished were appointed over these, and the whole were to obey the directions of a principal conductor, who took his place at the head of the column, with a bugleman to sound his orders. Such were the dispositions on the ground at Barrowfields. At the sound of the bugle not less than three thousand men formed a hollow square, with probably as many people around them, and, an impressive silence having been obtained, I reminded them that they were going to attend the most important meeting that had ever been held for Parliamentary Reform.' Banners boasting 'Unity and Strength' and 'Liberty and Fraternity' were carried to the accompaniment of a band. Weapons, such as staves, were discouraged. As the column marched towards Manchester it was joined by thousands more men, women and children.

When they reached the outskirts of Manchester, Bamford expected the column to be met by the local authorities who would read them the Riot Act, a proclamation made by the local magistrate in which a crowd was told to disperse or face military action as a result (the original Riot Act had been passed in 1715 to deal with Jacobite disturbances). Bamford overestimated the forethought of the Manchester authorities and no one prevented them from entering the city. Squeezing through the narrow streets in good order, they were met by other groups bearing banners such as 'Equal Representation or Death'. Bamford estimated there were some 80,000 people gathered in St. Peter's Field as Henry Hunt began to speak. It was now that the local authorities decided to act, perhaps panicked by the size and military overtones of the crowd. 'I stood on tip-toe,' recalled Bamford, 'and saw a party of cavalry in blue and white uniform come trotting, sword in hand, round the corner of the garden-wall, and to the front of a row of new houses, where they reined up in a line.' It was 40 members of the Manchester and Salford Yeomanry Cavalry, a militia unit.

'On the cavalry drawing up they were received with a shout of good-will,' says Bamford. 'They shouted again, waving their sabres over their heads; and then, slackening rein, and striking spur into their steeds, they

SCARLET TO KHAKI

For a good two hundred years, scarlet was the colour of the British Army, its red jackets being instantly recognisable from Canada to India, from South Africa to New Zealand. The 'Thin Red Line' was an enormously popular painting by Robert Gibb in 1881 showing the 93rd Highlanders withstanding an attack by Russian cavalry at the battle of Balaklava in the Crimean War. It had been inspired by the correspondent of The Times, William Russell, who originally described the combatants as a 'Thin Red Streak'. It became a Victorian icon, summing up the fighting spirit of the British soldier in the face of overwhelming odds. Ironically, however, within twenty years of this painting being completed, scarlet had been replaced by khaki as the dominant colour of the British Army uniform.

To view the Victorian army as a conservative organisation reluctant to face change is a complete misunderstanding of how it actually worked in practice. It was far more flexible and innovative than the armies of many other contemporary nations, a tendency derived from its colonial experience around the world. One of the fruits of this experience was the invention of khaki. Some early steps towards the use of camouflage had been made in North America when riflemen were clad in either green or grey, but in 1846 in India, a British officer called Harry Lumsden raised a unit of native infantry and cavalry in the Punjab and had them uniformed in loose fitting jackets and trousers coloured 'khaki', or 'drab', as it was then known. Khaki is an Urdu word meaning dusty or dust-coloured, coming from the Persian word for dust, khak. Drab is an English word derived from the Dutch

drab meaning dregs. The fashion spread among native soldiers in India and, during the Great Mutiny of 1857, several British units wore improvised uniforms made up of various forms of 'khaki' dyed with anything to hand such as tea, curry powder, or just dirt. This development was acknowledged officially by the Adjutant-General who ordered that 'for the future the summer clothing of the European soldiers shall consist of two suits of 'khakee'...'

The practicality of khaki was not, however, appreciated by many of the rank and file who preferred wearing their smart scarlet jackets, considering 'khaki' to be too scruffy to be seen in public. The government concurred, the order was countermanded and khaki disappeared officially for twenty years. With various other forms of camouflage being tested in colonial campaigns over the next few years, such as a grey-brown tweed jacket designed especially for fighting in the Ashanti War in 1873, khaki reappeared in 1885 as the standard service dress for the Indian Army and in 1896 this became universal for all service outside Europe, with the Boer War being the first major conflict in which the British went into battle in khaki. By 1902, khaki even superseded scarlet for home service and the British soldier had become very much a modern looking soldier.

The old gives way to the new with a Colour-Sergeant of the Gloucester Regiment in scarlet and a private in khaki; hand-coloured photograph taken around 1900. The British army was quite advanced in its adaption of a new more practical battledress for its soldiers at the beginning of the 20th century, years of colonial campaigning in all climates creating the experience that led to practical steps such as puttees, sun helmet, and khaki. [Peter Newark's Military Pictures]

'Britannia rules the Waves' says the caption to this contemporary print showing a royal salute off Spithead by the Royal Navy in 1886. With investment in new armoured steam-ships, the Royal Navy continued to dominate the sea right up to the First World War and even then the German navy could not compete in numbers with it, its presence deterring any thought of invading Britain. [Peter Newark's Military Pictures]

dashed forward and began cutting the people.' Panic amongst the demonstrators created a dense, seething crowd which prevented the horsemen from charging freely among them, although their sabres caused terrible injuries to the unprotected people stuck nearest to them. 'Their sabres were plied to hew a way through naked held-up hands and defenceless heads; and then chopped limbs and wound-gaping skulls were seen; and groans and cries were mingled with the din of that horrid confusion.'

Hunt and his supporters left the platform and the cavalry hacked down the banners surrounding it. 'On the breaking of the crowd the Yeomanry wheeled, and, dashing whenever there was an opening, they followed, pressing and wounding.' After ten minutes, the open space was empty, leaving only mounds of bodies, most of the injuries and deaths caused by trampling in the panic. Other sources claimed it was not the Yeomanry but regular cavalry held in reserve who caused the casualties, being used to rescue the Yeomanry who had become caught up in an angry crowd. At the end of the day, eleven people were dead and many hundreds injured. The subsequent support by the government for the decision of the magistrates caused a national outrage and gave additional moral force to the cause of the protesters which, with the Repeal of the Corn Laws, eventually succeeded.

The only armed insurrection to occur on British soil during this period was led by Sir William Courtenay, also known as Mad Tom, whose real name was John Tom. Indeed, it was the last battle ever to take place on English soil. It involved the regular British Army and the first officer to be killed in the reign of Queen Victoria.

The young queen had been on the throne for just a year in 1838 when dramatic events unfolded in Bossenden, Kent. John Tom had been a wine merchant and maltster in Truro, Cornwall, when he disappeared, leaving his old life behind. When he next appeared, in Canterbury in Kent, he had adopted a messianic character, wearing a full beard and long hair and proclaiming himself Count Moses

Rothschild. Receiving the financial support of local Jews, he set himself up as a champion of the oppressed, railing against tithes, taxes and an unfair government. He attracted a following and then changed his name to Sir William Courtenay, assuming the identity of a local land owner who had fled the country following a scandal and claiming his estates. He must have kept his eccentricity within the bounds of sanity for the Conservative party thought he might make a good candidate for MP, but in the following elections he received little real support. With this failure and the disillusionment of his patrons, the law caught up with John Tom, but rather than being transported, he was sent to Barming lunatic asylum where he spent the next five years.

John Tom was released from the lunatic asylum in 1837 but rather than stay with his father who had secured his release, he was accommodated by a wealthy farmer called George Francis. It was not long before he

Woodcut based on an eye-witness sketch of the battle in Bossenden Wood in Kent in 1838, the last battle fought on English soil, between Mad Tom and his club-wielding Kent farmers against the regular British Army of the 45th Foot. [Peter Newark's Military Pictures]

could see that the farm workers around him were not happy, the Poor Law Act having reduced their meagre pay even further. When he returned home with a brace of pistols, Francis became nervous and threw him out. Tom now acquired a white horse and rode round the country, saying he had been sent by God to free his Golden Ones, the poor of Kent. He quoted apocalyptic visions from the Book of Revelations, his speech being both threatening and seductive, as one contemporary witness recorded: 'He could turn men which way they liked, if they only once listened to him. A man I know could not sleep all Wednesday night, for thinking of him, and told his wife in the morning that he must go with Sir William; for if he did not, he was convinced that a shower of fire would come down from Heaven to burn him and his children to ashes.' His followers, numbering between 60 and 130, carried a flag bearing a red lion on a pale-blue background. They marched the roads around his base at Bossenden Farm and Tom declared it was time for a New Age which would be ushered in by rebellion.

The Gloucester Regiment at bayonet practice in 1896. The spiked helmet worn by these soldiers was copied from the pickelhaube introduced into the German army in the middle of the 19th century. At this time, before the later animosities of the 20th century, the German army was highly regarded for its successful wars against Austria and France and was seen as a model for other armies around the world, from Britain to Japan. [Peter Newark's Military Pictures]

A company barrack room photographed in 1897, neat and clean, ready for inspection. Spit and polish has long been an essential attribute of the British Army, reflecting both pride and discipline, fundamental for a soldier's effectiveness in battle. [Peter Newark's Military Pictures]

Fearing a riot or some other disturbance, the local Justice of the Peace issued a warrant for the arrest of Tom and his followers. It was to be served by constable John Mears, his brother Nicholas, and an assistant constable. When the arresting party arrived at Bossenden Farm, Tom approached the men and asked 'Are you the Constable?' When Nicholas Mears said 'yes', Tom pulled a pistol and shot him through the chest. The other two ran off and Tom returned to the wounded man, slashing him with his sword and shooting him again. The heavenly rebellion had begun and Tom and his men moved into Bossenden Wood to await the reaction of the authorities. A message went to the garrison at Canterbury Barracks and 100 soldiers of the 45th Foot with four officers responded. These were regular soldiers who had just returned from India. The commanding officer, Major Armstrong, decided to catch Tom in Bossenden Wood with a pincer movement, dividing his force into two detachments. The Justice of the Peace read the rebels the Riot Act and this legal formality having passed, Armstrong moved in.

John Tom and just one other of his supporters had guns, the rest were farming men wearing their traditional white smocks and armed with sticks used as clubs, but Tom had promised them heavenly support and they feared neither bullets nor bayonets. One detachment of soldiers, led by Lieutenant Bennett, did not wait for the bugle sounding the co-ordinated attack, but chose to advance into sight of Tom in a clearing in Bossenden Wood. Bennett, sword drawn, demanded that Tom surrender in the name of the Queen. Tom raised his pistol and shot Bennett dead, the first officer to die for

Queen Victoria. The rebels surged forward, but by now the second detachment had emerged out of the woods and joined the fight. A volley of musket-fire was delivered by Armstrong's detachment while the other soldiers, keen to avenge the death of their officer, used bayonet, butt and boot to fight the rebels with their cudgels. In the brief min-utes of combat, Tom and seven of his follow-ers were killed, while one constable who accompanied the soldiers was killed and many more badly wounded on both sides in the savage fight. With Tom dead, the rebels eventually broke.

Tom's body was taken to the nearby Red Lion pub to be put on display, but such was

the local belief in his divinity that many thought he would rise again on the third day and to scotch this, the coroner had his heart removed and pickled in a jar, which survived until the 1950s. Several of Tom's followers were arrested, tried and given sentences ranging from hard labour to transportation to Australia. The Red Lion pub is still very much as it was 150 years ago and contains a Courtenay lounge in memory of this bizarre rebellion. The performance of the rebels was seized upon by one correspondent for the Chambers Edinburgh Journal as an example of why British men were good at fighting: 'Nor do I believe there has ever been an instance in which a savage race, when they could not get at them hand to hand, have not been beaten by our men, unless when absolutely overwhelmed by numbers, as in the case of Sir Charles Macarthy's disaster in 1824 [against the Ashanti in west Africa]. The Kentish ploughmen who followed the impostor Tom, opposing their sticks to the muskets and bayonets of a more numerous body of soldiers, exhibited a much greater instance of courage than has ever been evinced by any foreign race. True, they were fanatics; but amongst what other fanatics, however besotted, can we discover such a manifestation of unflinching daring and nerve?'

Despite the sound defeat of Napoleonic France and the transformation of France from traditional enemy to new ally in the Crimean War, France still figured in the popular imagination as the main challenge Britain had to face in Europe. The Duke of Wellington had fuelled this fear in 1847 by declaring that the

Firing line of the recreated 1st Battalion, Middlesex Regiment. The soldiers are armed with the Mark II Martini-Henry Rifle, which was first introduced into service in 1876. It was the first purpose-built breechloading rifle for the British Army and replaced the Snider-Enfield. It could fire twelve rounds a minute and had an effective range of up to 400 yards. Experience shows that the Martini had a powerful recoil which got worse when the rifle was fouled and could break a man's collarbone if not handled properly. Prolonged firing made the barrel almost too hot to touch. [The Diehard Company]

invention of steam-powered ships meant that the traditional barrier of the English Channel could be breached within a week of war being declared. A debate waged between whether the British Navy was sufficient to defend against this threat or whether a new series of fortifications should be built. 'Immovable stations of defence, as a protection against invasion,' wrote Lord Dundonald, 'are not only costly and of doubtful utility, but a reliance on them is, in my mind, an indication of a declining state.' Nevertheless, the British government chose to switch money away from the navy towards a new series of expensive fortifications. A certain urgency was given to this process in the late 1850s when Napoleon III embraced a more aggressive foreign policy and rebuilt the port of Cherbourg for an enlarged and improved navy.

In 1859, Prime Minister Lord Palmerston oversaw a Royal Commission to analyse Britain's defences. It concluded that Britain's old defences were not good enough and that a whole new system needed to be created. 'If by a sudden attack an enemy landed in strength,' wrote the Prime Minister to his Chancellor, 'our Dockyards were to be destroyed our Maritime Power would more than half a century be paralysed and our Colonies, our Commerce, and the Subsistence of a large Part of our Population would be at the Mercy of our Enemy, who would be sure to shew us no Mercy - we should be reduced to the rank of a Third Rate Power if no worse happened to us.' He was convinced the Royal Navy would not be sufficient to stop such an attack and plans were drawn up to defend Portsmouth, the Isle of Wight, Spithead, Plymouth, Portland,

Pembroke, Dover, Chatham and the Medway. London was considered too vast to be defended. Nearly 12 million pounds was allocated to the project over four years. A total of 28 gun positions were built to defend Plymouth alone. Convict labour was used to construct a lot of the new forts which generally followed a similar plan of design, being either round or polygonal, surrounded by a ditch, with barracks inside. They were essentially gun platforms and the idea was not just to prevent a sea landing, but to bring fire to bear on a land army that attempted to capture a port, so many of their guns faced permanently inland. One of the best examples of these forts surviving today is the fully restored Fort Nelson at Portsmouth which houses the Royal Armouries collection of artillery as well as revealing the many underground passages and store-rooms that serviced the defences.

By 1870, Napoleon III's ambition to be the master of Europe was shown to be a sham. He was captured by the Prussians in a war which humiliated the French army, but a fear of French attack still continued in British planning circles and as late as 1891 a memorandum issued by the Secretary of State for War laid down the doctrine that the primary duty of the British Army was home defence, this policy holding until the Boer War in 1899. Such speculation was added to by French writers conceiving detailed invasion

Marching soldiers of the recreated 1st Battalion, Middlesex Regiment. They wear the undress 'frock' jacket which was the working dress of the day. It is faced with a white collar and cuffs reflecting the fact that it is an English regiment: Royal Regiments had blue facings, Scots Regiments yellow and Irish Regiments green. The white canvas haversack hanging from the right shoulder contained one day's rations. [The Diehard Company]

plans. In the Revue de Deux Mondes it was decided that a fleet of fifteen hundred armour-plated steam-powered barges would be sufficient to transport an army of some 150,000 men with 500 guns. The crossing would take just three or four hours under cover of night with the landing being covered by quick-firing guns in the bows of the barges. Such belligerence among the French served to mask the true threat to Britain which came from an increasingly powerful and recently united Germany.

The attitude of the British public to their army throughout the Victorian period was increasingly one of pride, as the number of British pubs named after battles in the Crimean War and other colonial conflicts clearly demonstrate. However, there was never any enthusiasm to pay for a bigger and better army through increased levels of taxation. Political pressure was constantly trying to reduce the amount of money spent on defence. This was in sharp contrast to the Prussian state where there was direct pressure from above to raise more and more money for a powerful army and navy that could dominate Europe and compete with Britain. The Duke of Wellington, commander in chief of the British Army for part of this period, had no problem in overseeing finan-

Sergeant of the recreated 1st Battalion, Middlesex Regiment, inspects his men while a drummer boy copies him. The soldiers wear the Home Service review order dress worn in 1886. The spiked helmet they wear was introduced in 1878 to replace the traditional shako worn since the Napoleonic Wars. It is copied from the German pickelhaube, reflecting a new interest in German military matters since their impressive victory over France in 1870. [The Diehard Company]

cial cuts from the major to the trivial: the army was reduced from a total of 220,000 men in 1815 to 94,500 in 1841, while the quality and quantity of lace worn by the 11th Hussars was also reduced, at a saving of £400 a year. The glory days of extravagantly uniformed soldiers was already past and a new practicality seized the army both in what the soldier wore and how he performed.

The mood of reduction and efficiency culminated in the reforms of Edward Cardwell, Secretary of State from 1868-74. Some regiments were amalgamated, all lost their old numbers, and each new regiment was organised into two battalions linked to areas in Britain where they had their home depot and from which they were expected to recruit. The idea was to give a more local character to each battalion. One battalion would serve abroad while the other battalion stayed at home, ever ready to feed new recruits abroad when needed. Active service was reduced to six years but with a further six years spent in the reserve, again to build up a trained body

of men that could be called upon in an emergency without having the cost of supporting a large standing army. Colonial garrisons were withdrawn from countries of the Empire such as Canada, Australia and New Zealand which were now expected to defend themselves at their own expense. The tradition of officers purchasing their way into the army was abolished and the commander in chief became a subordinate adviser to the Secretary of State. Unfortunately, it was considered that the short service terms meant that British soldiers were less experienced and because army pay did not rise to match that in the civil sector it did not attract the most talented people. Conscription, a thoroughly European solution to falling recruitment, was never enacted in Britain in the Victorian era.

A typical military unit of the Victorian era has been recreated recently by the award-winning re-enactment group the Diehard Company. The history of this unit gives an idea of the range of service expected from a typical Victorian battalion and the way an average British serviceman could end up travelling the world. Beginning as the 57th Foot during the Napoleonic Wars, they won their famous nickname at the battle of Albuera in Spain in 1811 when they lost 22 out of 25 officers and 425 other ranks killed and wounded out of 570. Their commander, Colonel Inglis, lying wounded in front of them, ordered his men to: 'Die hard my boys, die hard!' From 1831 to 1846, the 57th saw service in India. It then returned home for garrison duty until 1853 when it sailed to Corfu and then to the Crimea in southern Russia where it fought at Balaklava, Inkerman and the Redan. It was garrisoned in Malta until 1858 when it was transferred to India to help secure the country after the Great Mutiny. In 1860, it sailed from India to New Zealand where it took part in the Maori Wars. In 1874, it moved to Ceylon and then to South Africa where it fought against the Zulus, returning home in 1879. In 1881, following the Cardwell reforms, the 57th was amalgamated with the 77th Regiment and became the 1st Battalion, Middlesex Regiment, with its regimental depot at Hounslow Barracks.

The Victorian era saw a technological revolution in the Royal Navy in which wooden sailing-ships were superseded by steel-clad, steam-powered battleships firing shells some twenty times further than the cannons of Nelson's fleet. The French added to the alarm of the British not only by talking about how easy it was to cross the Channel by steam-boat but also by building in 1860 the first armoured ocean-going warship, the Gloire. Britain responded by initiating the Warrior, a massive iron battleship second only in size to the Great Eastern and almost twice as long, twice as heavy and twice as powerful as the Gloire, being armed with forty 68-pounder guns. It was completed in 1861 and had such a durable structure that it can still be seen today afloat at Portsmouth where it has been fully restored. HMS Warrior caught the popular imagination and coincided with a new public interest in the navy and its sailors. No longer viewed solely as drunken trouble-makers forced into service, the heroic involvement of Naval Brigades in colonial actions abroad stimulated popular fiction and music-hall songs and Jolly Jack Tar became a selling point in advertising for Victorian commodities such as tobacco and soap.

In the wake of the Warrior, an international naval arms race began in which bigger and stronger ships competed with more powerful guns. Guns were armoured in turrets and placed on turntables. Sails disappeared completely and steel took over from iron, being both lighter and stronger. Torpedoes and machine-guns were added to the armoury. Such developments cost an enormous amount of money and the British government began to rein back on expenditure from 1870 to 1890, but by then France had been displaced by Germany as the main European threat and a new naval race began, cumulating in the construction of the Dreadnought in 1906, the first big-gun battleship of the 20th century with ten 12 inch guns and turbine propulsion. Britain had entered the modern age of warfare and the effects of this on its people and its soldiers would be demonstrated in 1914 with the outbreak of the First World War.

Recreating the appearance of a trench on the Western Front, members of The Great War Society wear a variety of clothing, such as leather jackets, introduced to cope with fighting in the cold, wet terrain. [Great War Society]

TOMMIES
AND POPPIES

*After decades of colonial 'small wars', the British Army
was deployed to France in 1914 to resist the German invasion.
After four years of unprecedented bloodshed, the British and
their allies won a series of victories in 1918 that ended the war.*

The Great War began in 1914 like any other war involving Britain over the previous hundred years. A small professional expeditionary force was sent abroad and the British public read about their heroic achievements in the newspapers. This war, however, would prove to be very different. The initial optimism of the British public would be tested to the limit as the casualties grew from thousands to tens of thousands to hundreds of thousands and more. The Great War or First World War was the first continental war Britain had fought since the struggle against Napoleon and it demanded a scale of involvement previously unknown to the British people.

Within three months, the British Expeditionary Force of 160,000 was exhausted and nearly wiped out. It had fought well and stopped the German line of advance in Belgium, but whereas Germany and France used conscription to raise armies of millions, the British reserve system and the Territorial army could not match their numbers. In Britain, conscription smacked of Continental tyranny and the government preferred to rely on volunteers to fill the ranks. As War Minister, Field Marshal Kitchener initiated a

The famous poster featuring Field Marshal Kitchener, Secretary of State for War, encouraging hundreds of thousands of men to volunteer to join the British Army in 1914. [Peter Newark's Military Pictures]

massive new recruitment drive in which posters were used featuring him pointing at the viewer, declaring 'Your Country needs YOU!' It was an enormous success with some 761,000 men joining up in the first eight weeks. By 1915, five new armies were raised and Britain could fight with Germany on more equal terms. Some volunteers came from the Territorial Army, but there were also older, family men among these soldiers and those who did not volunteer to fight abroad were incorporated into a Home Defence Force.

The new volunteers served in what were known as Kitchener battalions which were attached to the regular battalions of the British Army. Many men volunteered together with their friends and these units based on local ties were known as Pals battalions. The path by which these new soldiers entered the war has been recorded by a group of researchers at the University of Reading who have focused on one group of locals in Reading. In their case, the appeal for volunteers began in August 1914 with announcements in the local press asking for all able-bodied men between 19 and 30 to come forward and enlist. Kitchener representatives also addressed meetings at local factories and the Town Hall. On September 5th, the Reading Standard reported that in just two days nearly 1,000 men had enlisted. The flood of volunteers overwhelmed the depot of the Royal Berkshire Regiment which was used to handling some 300 men but not the 2,000 they had at one stage. Local council members protested, saying the recruits should be 'treated like human beings' and be given sufficient food and sleeping accommodation.

By October, recruiting in Reading had slowed down and the barracks had processed the new men. Some even enjoyed temporary billets in hotels, setting up a canteen in the Palm Court. Officers had to equip themselves quickly. 'We rushed to Moss Bros, the military outfitters in Covent Garden,' remembered subaltern Patrick Gold, 'and a frantic buying spree commenced: cap badge, tunic, slacks, breeches, puttees, boots, socks, greatcoat, sword, kitbag, camp-beds, khaki shirts, ties, handkerchiefs, compasses, revolver and holster and a host of other minor things.'

Training for the first Kitchener battalions of the Royal Berkshire Regiment began at Shorncliffe near Folkestone on the south coast. It was a simple process, as Private Harding records: 'The rifle, with courses of target practice at Hythe Ranges and plenty of full-pack marching, plus square-bashing, certainly got us very fit.' By the following spring, these new recruits were embarked on ships and arrived at Boulogne at the end of May 1915. They were then transported to Ploegsteert in Belgium where they immediately became part of the great system of trenches that stretched from the North Sea to Switzerland and so defined the fighting on the Western Front for the next three years. 'We went straight to the front,' recalls George Strong who joined in Reading at the age of 18, 'I remember Rutoir Farm and the Guards coming out of the line. One of them said to me: 'Can you swim lad? The conditions are 'orrible.'

All over the country, a similar story could be told, with young farm labourers and factory workers leaving their jobs and families behind to serve in the mud of Flanders and

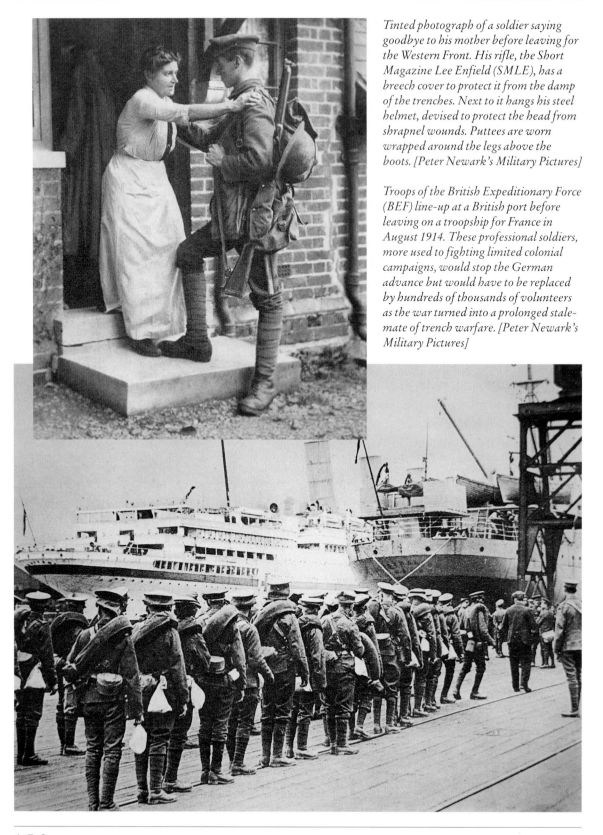

Tinted photograph of a soldier saying goodbye to his mother before leaving for the Western Front. His rifle, the Short Magazine Lee Enfield (SMLE), has a breech cover to protect it from the damp of the trenches. Next to it hangs his steel helmet, devised to protect the head from shrapnel wounds. Puttees are worn wrapped around the legs above the boots. [Peter Newark's Military Pictures]

Troops of the British Expeditionary Force (BEF) line-up at a British port before leaving on a troopship for France in August 1914. These professional soldiers, more used to fighting limited colonial campaigns, would stop the German advance but would have to be replaced by hundreds of thousands of volunteers as the war turned into a prolonged stalemate of trench warfare. [Peter Newark's Military Pictures]

France. By 1916, even these volunteers were not enough and conscription was reluctantly introduced. The drain on manpower in Britain was significant, depriving British industry of much needed labour. The result was to increase the proportion of women in work. Before the war, the majority of working women in Britain were employed as domestic servants or in the textile industry. As the war progressed, women began to work in manufacturing, commerce, government, education, and public transport. Above all, the expanding munitions industry needed women workers and by the end of the war almost a million women were employed. These were skilled, higher paid jobs giving women a taste of independence which they might not have had but for the war.

Women also worked directly for the armed services. There were some 23,000 nurses working in military hospitals in Britain, while the First Aid Nursing Yeomanry (FANY) trained nurses to serve on the battlefield. The Women's Emergency League trained army cadets in signalling, while the Women's Auxiliary Force trained part-time workers in helping with canteens, entertainment and air-raid shelters. In 1917, women donned uniforms for the first time in British history to serve in the Women's Army Auxiliary Corps (WAAC) where they worked as cooks, drivers, and typists, the Women's Royal Naval Service (WRNS) working as signallers as well as making mine nets and preparing torpedoes, and, in 1918, the Women's Royal Air Force (WRAF) where they were employed as drivers and fitters.

As for the men, some 5.7 million men served in the armed forces out of a population of 46.4 million. It was a war unlike any other war in the history of Britain. It has been called the first total war and it certainly affected every aspect of life in the country. Politics was supposedly suspended for the duration of the war with all parties working together, but the dreadful casualties in the battle of the Somme in 1916 and increased shipping losses from German U-boats forced Prime Minister Asquith to resign. He was replaced by Lloyd George, who constantly disagreed with the strategy of the British commander in chief, Field Marshal Haig.

Government control extended over industry with Lloyd George personally leading a campaign to increase the amount of artillery shells produced. His War Contracts Office expanded from a staff of twenty to 65,000. As a result, Britain produced 5,090,442 rifles, 239,840 machine-guns, 25,031 artillery guns, 2,818 tanks, and 54,798 aircraft. So efficient was the British economy that it actually produced a great deal of material for the French as well who had lost many of their industrial regions in the early days of the war. The price of all this was crippling and whereas most foreign governments paid for the war through borrowing and printing money, thus putting up inflation, Britain put the burden on taxation, raising income tax to 30 per cent of income, but at least avoiding the severe economic problems that would later face countries such as Germany once the war was over.

That a war should have such an enormous impact on Britain was extraordinary enough but especially so when one considers that it was fought abroad. Britain largely avoided the ravages of war on its own land, although it did not escape totally unscathed. Earlier fears of a Continental invasion were revived in 1914 when German Rear Admiral Franz Hipper sailed his battle cruisers towards the British coast. In early November, they shelled Yarmouth and laid a series of mines in the way of coastal shipping. A month later, they bombarded Hartlepool, Whitby and Scarborough, causing considerable damage, killing forty civilians and injuring many more. Fortuitously, a few months earlier, a German light cruiser had run aground in Estonia and the Russians passed a German naval code book on to the British navy. Using this breakthrough to decode the plans of the Germans, the Royal Navy cruised off Dogger Bank in the North Sea, waiting to intercept the returning German raiders. Bad weather prevented the Royal Navy from engaging with the German ships and the opportunity was lost to avenge the assault on Britain's coast but it nevertheless achieved a tremendous amount in propaganda, with newspapers portraying the Germans as the 'baby killers of Scarborough', thus stiffening British resolve.

Before the war, many novelists had depicted a war of the future in which new technology would mean that war could be fought with airships and aircraft. With only a handful of observation aircraft in service at the beginning of the war, it seemed a bit far-fetched, but by 1915 this particular form of science fiction came true when on January 19th a series of giant rigid airships called Zeppelins appeared over Britain and dropped bombs on civilian targets. The raids culminated in the largest airborne assault against London on October 13th. In a recollection recorded by the Imperial War Museum, Margaret Warren, a nurse, narrowly missed one such raid: 'I remember one bad one in Leicester Square. I had been there the week before and had a marvellous time. The week after that the whole place was bombed to small pieces. Some Zeppelin had come along and bumped them off. Several of my friends were there which was very sad. That rather shook me. One girl in particular, a friend of mine, was told not to go up to London that particular day

because she wasn't well enough, she had flu, but she went and was killed.'

Launched from sites in Belgium, these Zeppelins could carry bomb loads of over 1,200 kg and reach high altitudes, conducting their air-raids from above the clouds. Britain suffered some 51 Zeppelin raids with half of them in 1916. Some 196 tons of bombs were dropped and 557 people were killed with 1,358 wounded. It was estimated that they caused one and a half million pounds worth of damage to property. Anti-aircraft measures were devised, including searchlight batteries, blackouts of civilian lights, anti-aircraft guns and an extensive air-raid shelter system. By 1917, however, British fighter aircraft had improved considerably and the giant Zeppelins became increasingly vulnerable to attack, especially from incendiary bullets which ignited the hydrogen-filled balloons. 'They put beautiful searchlights on it,' recalls Annie Howell, a gas mask factory worker who saw one such aerial combat. 'It [the Zeppelin] was all solid silver. Then in all different directions came shafts of light, about five of them. Of course they shot it down. The sight was magnificent if you'd never seen it before, but I thought at the time all those poor men in it.' Their German commanders considered the losses worth the effect on civilian morale. In reality, however,

Lieutenant W. L. Robinson shoots down a Zeppelin during a German air-raid over England on the night of September 2nd 1916 and wins a Victoria Cross. Searchlights from below have illuminated the airship while it drops its bombs, making it a vulnerable target. Contemporary painting by W. Avis. [Peter Newark's Military Pictures]

it only outraged British public opinion further. In 1918, strategic bombing dwindled to only four air-raids on Britain.

If warfare could now be fought in the skies above Britain, new technology also enabled an enemy to impinge on its coastal waters with the introduction of effective submarines. On February 4th, 1915, the German government declared the sea around Britain and Ireland, including the English Channel, to be a war zone in which German submarines, or U-boats as they became known, could destroy any merchant ship or civilian vessel without warning. This included pas-

Members of the award-winning British First World War re-enactment group, The Great War Society, line up in front of a surviving British tank of the period. By 1916, British soldiers had begun to develop combined arms tactics in which soldiers operated alongside artillery and the newly developed tanks to overcome the deep defensive lines of the Western Front. Each soldier wears a gas mask in the bag hanging on his chest to protect against devastating gas attacks launched by the German army. [Great War Society]

Food shortages were caused in Britain by German submarines sinking hundreds of British and American supply ships in the Atlantic and rationing had to be introduced towards the end of the war. It was an aspect of total warfare that British civilians had not experienced before. [Peter Newark's Military Pictures]

Women Volunteers for Defence march through London. Several organisations involving women helping the war effort were created during the First World War. They mainly helped in support roles, serving as nurses, drivers, and military secretaries, freeing men to fight in the frontline. [Peter Newark's Military Pictures]

senger liners and the subsequent loss of civilian life was tremendous. The Germans justified the act by saying that the British naval blockade on goods entering Germany demanded a similar response. But almost instantly, the move backfired.

On May 1st, 1915, one of the two largest passenger liners operating between Britain and the United States, the Lusitania, was intercepted by three U-boats south of Ireland and torpedoed. A total of 1,201 civilian passengers drowned. 124 of the passengers were Americans. This caused a tremendous outcry in the United States. President Wilson declined to declare war, but the reality of the European conflict had now touched the American people directly and this would make it easier for them to enter the war in 1917. In the meantime, Britain suffered terribly from U-boat attacks. In 1915, some 748,000 tons of British shipping was sunk. It brought pressure to bear on Britain's economy and the Germans were convinced that if they stepped up this unrestricted campaign they would ultimately win the war at sea, if not on land. Political pressure, however, and the desire not to antagonise the United States any further, brought a reduction in the campaign, with a promise not to sink merchant shipping without warning and to ensure passengers were provided for. Thus, unrestricted submarine warfare came to an end.

Zeppelin and U-boat raids gave the British public only a hint of what was happening over the Channel in Belgium and France. This public had been raised on the wars of empire and these gave no indication of the horror now facing British men in the trenches. 1916 was the lowest point for the conduct of war on the Western Front. At the battle of the

Somme, on just the first day, some 60,000 British soldiers became casualties, a third of them killed, the greatest one-day loss in the history of the British Army. As news of deaths of loved ones reached home, accompanied by long lines of wounded, a depressed mood took hold of Britain. There was no longer the 1914 optimism of victory by Christmas, with men joining up quickly before it was all over. In 1916, conscription had to be introduced. This was a war that looked as though it might go on forever, until both sides ran out of young men to fight it. That public opinion did not wholly turn against the war effort was in part due to both an innate sense of duty which the majority of people had grown up with and the role of the media which lessened the impact of the war through censorship. There were no news reels of wounded soldiers cowering in trenches, no photographs of bloated corpses in no-man's land.

Woman operator in munitions factory. With male factory workers volunteering to fight on the Western Front, vital industries supplying ammunition turned to women to operate the machines, greatly expanding the number of women working in traditionally male-dominated industries. [Peter Newark's Military Pictures]

A handful of war correspondents were accompanied by officers on the Western Front and they had no intention of reporting news that might undermine the morale of those at home. 'We identified ourselves absolutely with the army in the field,' declared Philip Gibbs of the Daily Telegraph. 'There was no need of censorship of our despatches. We were our own censors.' On top of this, editorial views at home helped to further the impression that, though it was a tough war, Britain and her allies would eventually triumph. Sometimes, journalists presented a completely

false picture. Charles Lowe of the Illustrated London News described the wounded after of the battle of Neuve Chapelle thus: 'the cheeriest crowd of wounded ever seen with the fierce joy of strife sparkling in their eyes.' Sometimes journalists even made up fantastic stories, such as the account of the Angels of Mons, when it was said that the ghosts of the archers of the Hundred Years War could be seen in the skies helping the soldiers on the Western Front. Later, Arthur Machen admitted he had fabricated the story to cheer up his readers, although many people continued to believe the vision was true.

Anger at the war-mongering Germans was maintained in the minds of many British by the reporting of German war atrocities.

Much of this has been dismissed as crude propaganda, but recent research has revealed that the German army did consider the brutal treatment of civilians a legitimate part of the way to conduct an effective war. Many accounts of Belgian civilians massacred by German soldiers, their towns looted and destroyed were in fact true. Savage cartoons, especially by the Dutchman Louis Raemaeker, who had to flee Holland because a price had been put on his head by the Germans, enhanced these accounts of barbarism. With reports of German war atrocities overwhelming more restrained descriptions of Britain's own losses, a sense of outrage was one more ingredient in British resolve to carry on the war, despite the horrendous casualties.

The Great War came to an end in 1918 with a series of victories won by the British Army against the Germans in what is now called the Hundred Days. It began with a counter-offensive against the German spring attack which had initially sent the Allies reeling backwards. Great improvements in tactics and equipment helped the British soldiers score victory after victory against the exhausted German Army which now began to collapse. By November, the war was over. It was a cause for celebration in 1918, but ever after it has never really been treated as such. The names of the Great War battles do not survive in our memory like Waterloo or

Recreated First World War troops pose in front of a surviving Thornycroft lorry. Although mechanised vehicles did make an impact on the conduct of war on the Western Front, horses were still by far the most common means of transport. [Great War Society]

Recreated First World War soldiers sit on a surviving Simplex Loco trench railway train. This was an ingenious response to the problem of carrying tons of supplies and ammunition along the miles of trenches on the Western Front. [Great War Society]

Trafalgar. Only the Somme and Passchendaele strike a chord in our collective memory, and only then because of the scale of the sacrifice. Why did a notably pugnacious people such as the British suddenly take no pride in their military achievement?

For hundreds of years, Britons had rejoiced in a string of successes unparalleled in the history of any other nation's warfare. In the years after 1918, however, pride in this military past deflated. The total casualties suffered by the British Empire in the Great War amounted to almost a million soldiers dead and two million wounded. Some 30,000 civilians were killed, two thirds being the victims of German submarines. Not only were many families touched by these losses, but sometimes whole villages were decimated

when the destruction of a Pals battalion meant that losses were concentrated in one particular area. The wounded struggled in civilian life to obtain jobs and lead normal lives. There was a great determination that losses on this scale should never be forgotten. War memorials were erected in almost every town across Britain and November 11th, the day of the Armistice in 1918, was declared a day of Remembrance in which wreathes of flowers, especially poppies, would be laid before the war memorials, and a minute's silence observed throughout the country. Sobre reflection rather than jubilant triumph was the order of the day and continues to be the tone observed to the present.

The scale of human losses allied with the enormous material cost of defeating

Soldiers of the Queen's Own Royal West Kent Regiment relax before a tent during an exercise in England on the eve of the First World War. Soldiers such as this formed the British Expeditionary Force that sailed to Belgium in 1914 to face the invading German army. [Peter Newark's Military Pictures]

WAR MEMORIALS

The loss of life in the Great War was so large and touched so many families that the British public demanded a way in which they could honour the memory of all those that had died. In previous wars, occasional statues were raised to eminent generals or remarkable victories, but more often than not the ordinary soldier was buried where he fell, often in an unmarked grave. This would not happen to those soldiers that had died on the Western Front. All the remains that could be traced were gathered together in special cemeteries along the Western Front with each soldier's grave marked by an individual stone with an inscription chosen by his family. The cemeteries continue to be tended today and provide a destination for those who wish to know a little of how their relatives died.

In Britain, debate ensued on the best way to remember the names of men lost to communities whose bodies were buried abroad. Some suggested that hospitals or funds should be initiated in their memory and these plans were followed through, although eighty years later little now remains of many of these schemes. The most abiding and effective war memorials today are those raised in stone or bronze which can be found in almost every village, town and city in Britain. Some are striking military figures in bronze, others are just stone plaques, but all of them make great effort to list all the names of those who died from each particular community. They act as focal points for acts of remembrance each November.

An exhibition of models and drawings by great artists of the time was shown at the Royal Academy in London in 1919 to help communities decide on the form their memorials should take. Most of the money to build these memorials was raised locally. Usually the dates appearing on the memorials are 1914 to 1918, but some include 1919 as Peace Day was officially celebrated in Britain on July 19th 1919. Occasionally, a man's name might appear on a memorial who had not died, but more often than not names were mistakenly left off and continued to be added for years after. A few memorials were raised to the animals, especially horses, who died during the war. One memorial on the edge of a golf course in Southampton records: 'Warrior. This White Gelding, 16 hands, served with the Old Contemptibles in France from 1914 to the end of the war. He took part in the retreat from Mons and was wounded in the advance on the Aisne. After the shrapnel had been extracted he returned to duty and did service in several further actions until the armistice.'

One of the most effective war memorials was that created by the sculptor Charles Sargeant Jagger for the Royal Artillery

Bronze figure of a Royal Artillery horse driver on the Jagger memorial. From the outspread ground sheet worn as a poncho to the armour plate attached to his leg to protect him against the wood of the gun carriage while riding the lead horse, it is a fully authentic representation of a soldier on the frontline. [Peter Newark's Military Pictures]

IN PROUD REMEMBRANCE OF THE
FORTY NINE THOUSAND & SEVENTY SIX
OF ALL RANKS OF THE
ROYAL REGIMENT OF ARTILLERY
WHO GAVE THEIR LIVES FOR KING
AND COUNTRY IN THE GREAT WAR
1914 - 1919

...USSIA · PALEST... CENTRAL ASIA

which stands near Hyde Park Corner in central London. Erected in 1925 in memory of the 49,076 dead of the Royal Artillery, it takes the form of a giant stone howitzer surrounded by four massive soldiers cast in bronze. One of the soldiers lies dead with his coat and helmet covering his face and chest, while the three other soldiers represent in detail some of the equipment worn by artillerymen, such as overalls used to carry shells, capes to ward off the rain, and armour worn to protect the legs while riding horses pulling guns. Stone reliefs to the side of them reflect some of the chaos and sacrifice of combat. Its combination of artistry and authenticity stands out above many other memorials which instead chose idealised views of the soldiers that died. Jagger's massive figures convey the heroism of the soldiers through the burdens they carried both in life and in spirit. It is the way soldiers themselves would wish to be remembered.

Royal Artillery Memorial by Charles Sargeant Jagger at Hyde Park Corner, London. Erected in 1925, this impressive war memorial to the dead of the First World War, is made of stone with bronze statues of artillerymen. It is said of the stone howitzer that if it were fired from this position, with sufficient charge, the shell would land on the Somme. [Peter Newark's Military Pictures]

Members of The Great War Society create a living war memorial to the dead of the First World War in a service at St. Symphorien Cemetery, near Mons in Belgium. Extensive new war cemeteries were created in Belgium and France shortly after the end of the First World War as a focal point for the grief felt by British civilians who wished to visit the battlefields where their loved ones had died. [Great War Society]

Germany caused many people to wonder at the wisdom of fighting the war at all. Prime Minister Lloyd George wrote memoirs in which he managed to shift the blame for the conduct of the war from the politicians to the generals, forever condemning Haig and his generals as incompetent commanders whose out of date views contributed to unnecessary losses. Certainly, the British high command had taken some time to come to terms with the enormous scale of the war against Germany, but they had been the first to say it would not be an easy task and that considerable casualties should be expected. By 1916, they had embraced new technology and new tactics and their skill in adapting a small colonial expeditionary force to a modern continental war did result in Germany's

defeat. The post-war mood, however, was one of cynicism. The victory did not resolve the balance of power in Continental Europe, economic depression followed, and only twenty years later, Germany would launch another devastating war. The real nature of modern warfare was also revealed in a series of graphic autobiographies and poems written by soldiers who had experienced the appalling conditions of the Western Front and were no longer constrained by war-time censorship. From the 1920s onwards, fewer and fewer people believed in the glamour of war. Not only had the scarlet uniforms of Wellington's day given way to drab khaki, but the scale and cost of warfare had changed forever.

DAD'S ARMY
AND THE BLITZ

With the defeat of France in June 1940 and the evacuation of the BEF from Dunkirk, Britain faced its most serious invasion threat since the eighteenth century. German army plans included the landing of Rommel's 7th panzer division on the coast of Kent.

The Great War should have been the war to end all wars. Most people considered such destruction could never happen again; no sane person could set in motion the events leading to world war. A majority of politicians in Britain favoured peace at any price, a policy that became known as appeasement, but Winston

Londoners sleeping on the platform of the Elephant and Castle Underground station in November 1940 during the Blitz. Tube stations were the only deep underground shelters against bombing raids available to the civilian population and were very popular, eventually being organised with bunks and trains providing food. [Peter Newark's Military Pictures]

Churchill thought it equally insane to ignore the possibility of another war with Germany and urged massive rearmament. Other people in Britain also considered it prudent to prepare for the worse and they took action by digging. The Zeppelin raids of the First World War had alerted Britain's military command to the potentially devastating impact of air-raids on the ability of a country to survive a war. By the 1920s, airpower had grown in strength and range and the War Office initiated a project to house ammunition deep below ground.

The subterranean project centred on quar-

Poster produced in 1939 showing the vital role of air-raid wardens. Civilian volunteers served in their thousands in this role, spotting for bomb damage and fire and ensuring that the rest of the population observed the strict air-raid rules, such as keeping a blackout in their houses. [Peter Newark's Military Pictures]

ries in Corsham in Wiltshire which had been used for years to dig out the stone used for the honey-coloured Georgian buildings of nearby Bath. It began in 1928 as a six acre secure storage depot for some 12,000 tons of shells and bombs at a cost of 100,000 pounds, but as the threat of war grew in the 1930s, ambitions grew for this maze of tunnels and caverns and by 1943 it became a complete underground town covering 125 acres, housing 300,000 tons of explosives and costing over four and a half million pounds. 'Many thousands of lights burn continuously in this land of hidden cities,' wrote a journalist in the Daily Express, finally revealing the nature of this defensive measure to his wartime readers. 'Warm conditioned air flows

through arterial channels of concrete and limestone. Shells painted a gay yellow rock endlessly on a conveyor belt, to be stacked in a twenty-foot honey-comb, or to be shipped to a theatre of war. Here, carved from the living rock, is a great bomb-proof cloister hundreds of feet long, supported by square thirty-foot columns hewn out of stone. Already scurrying blobs of khaki have piled it high with war stores. And here on rock covered with smooth concrete, engineers have built a great powerhouse, with whirring giant dynamos, winking signal lights and shiny black controls. Fluorescent bars throw a daylight effect over the spotless asphalt floors.' The intention of revealing this during wartime was no doubt to convey to the

Germans the futility of continuing bombing raids against British targets.

Excavation of these underground shelters was enormously demanding in labour and money. Thousands of labourers were employed, but when war came, these men were needed in the army and a recruiting office was opened in Dublin and over 10,000 Irish labourers came to Britain. With a reputation for hard-drinking, they were not exactly welcomed in the sleepy West Country villages around Corsham and the government had to consider plans to build eight camps equipped with canteens, bars and cinemas. Aside from quarrying, some of the tunnels had been used for mushroom farming and as work progressed other activities were discovered. In one corner, concealed behind rows of rotting mushroom shelves, a die-press was discovered with a considerable amount of counterfeit half-crown coins. The people involved were later arrested and imprisoned.

Such preparation meant that when war came, Britain's ammunition was safely stored in extensive shelters beneath Wiltshire, Staffordshire and Caernarvonshire. The subterranean chambers were also used to store other valuable commodities, such as antiquities and art evacuated from the British Museum and the National Gallery, state archives from several East European governments in exile, and tens of millions of French francs to replace the German currency imposed on the invaded French nation. More valuable, however, was the preservation of Britain's industrial production and wartime plans were made to house entire factories underground so that aircraft could continue to be built to defend Britain against German air-raids. The Treasury was horrified at the expense this would entail, but Churchill, by then Prime Minister, was enthusiastic and the biggest scheme was begun at Spring Quarry near Corsham with a myriad of underground chambers incorporating machine shops,

Although chemical warfare was not used against the British during the Blitz, it remained a terrifying threat and whole families were provided with gasmasks. [Peter Newark's Military Pictures]

stores of raw materials, offices, canteens, and hostels for workers. McAlpine won the contract worth seven million pounds and BAC was intended to occupy the factory, carrying out airframe construction and engine development with some 2,000 factory workers housed underground. Eventually, with the reduction of German air-raids, the scheme was down-sized, but it still cost millions of pounds and became known as Beaverbrook's folly, after the minister in charge of the project.

The threat of invasion to Britain was never stronger in the 20th century than in 1940. The German army had stormed through Poland, Norway, Denmark, Holland, Belgium and France, its motorised columns giving a new dynamism to warfare which had been missing in the First World War. British and French troops failed to hold the Germans as they had before along the Western Front. France surrendered in June 1940 while the British

Expeditionary Force was forced to evacuate the Continent at Dunkirk. Adolf Hitler, supreme commander of the German army, now turned his gaze across the Channel and ordered his generals to prepare for an invasion of Britain which would be called Operation Sea Lion. Detailed plans were drawn up for an invasion which would land at Dover in Kent and send armoured spearheads racing through the Home Counties until Panzer divisions had neutralised Britain's military divisions and surrounded London. It all seemed very likely and never more so since Britain seemed so unprepared.

The Royal Navy was still a force to be reckoned with and, like Napoleon and Philip II before him, Hitler knew he could not compete directly with it. His breakthrough would be to use his formidable airforce of fighters, dive-bombers and bombers to destroy the RAF and then turn it on the Royal Navy. With both these arms

During the Battle of Britain in 1940, the frontline against Nazi Germany was in the skies above England. The Spitfire fighter airplane shown here, along with the Hurricane, were the main weapons used by the RAF against the greater numbers of German bombers and fighters that fought to destroy British airpower in preparation for Hitler's invasion of the country.
[Peter Newark's Military Pictures]

out of the way, it would then be relatively straight forward to defeat the British on land. The battle for Britain would be won in the air or not at all. Hermann Goering was the head of the German Luftwaffe and entrusted with this vital task. Using airfields in the conquered lands of France, Belgium, Holland and Norway, the British Isles were within the range of all of his aircraft and he was highly confident of victory.

The campaign began with testing raids on British shipping and coastal towns, then, in August 1940, the first massive air attack began. For ten days, from August 8th, some 900 German fighters and 1,300 bombers flew over 1,000 sorties every day and night. They targeted English air bases and seaports, hoping to shoot the British aircraft down as they flew out to defend these vital points. The British RAF was outnumbered almost four to one, able to muster only some 650 fighters, although among them were the legendary Spitfire and Hurricane aircraft. Science came to their aid in the form of radar which had been recently devised, allowing the RAF to have advanced warning of where exactly the German airplanes were attacking and so could use its smaller airforce more precisely and effectively to meet these attacks. The result was that after ten days, the Luftwaffe had failed to break the British air defence.

RATIONING

The Second World War was a total war in the sense that it was not fought just between armies but between whole nations, soldiers and civilians both being part of the overall war effort. It was a war of economies and the Germans used submarines to sink ships bringing food and other supplies to Britain from North America. As a result of this, there were shortages of basic foods and commodities and rationing had to be introduced to ensure that everyone had a fair share of what arrived in the country. Bacon, butter, sugar, tea, cheese, cooking fat, jam, eggs and sweets were all rationed, with coupons being exchanged for a set amount of each of these per week. Further coupons were provided on a points system, allowing people to buy different kinds of food. A tin of salmon was worth sixteen points, but that was a whole month's allocation of points. Foreign fruits such as bananas were unavailable. Tobacco and alcohol were never rationed but the price of bottles of beer or whisky rose sharply, more than doubling in price.

In order to help the public make the most of the dire situation, government advisers came up with ideas for recipes using more readily available foods such as carrots and potatoes. Shredded carrot was recommended as a natural sweetener, to be added to puddings and cakes, while Minister for Food Lord Woolton gave his name to a pie made from potatoes, carrots, turnips and parsnips baked in a pastry, although many

people considered it a 'steak and kidney pie without the steak and kidney'. More successful as a substitute for fresh meat was Spam, a form of processed pork, which derived its name from Supply Pressed American Meat. It arrived in tins from America and could be sliced and fried and served in a variety of ways, although the Strand Palace Hotel was probably pushing it too far when it gave a Spam dish the French name of 'ballotine de jambon Valentinoise'.

Weekly war rations for two people in Britain in 1941, painted by Leonora K. Green. The battle for the Atlantic in which German submarines sank hundreds of British and American supply ships meant that food shortages became ever more severe until combined actions involving aircraft and battleships turned the tide against the U-boats, eventually bringing their campaign to an end. [Peter Newark's Military Pictures]

After a brief pause, a second massive attack began at the end of August, running through to September 5th. Groups of bombers escorted by fighters concentrated on attacking the major inland RAF bases. It was a devastating assault, destroying some 450 British fighters. Britain responded by throwing its bombers against Germany, launching its first raids on the German capital. This infuriated Hitler who instructed Goering to shift his attack away from the airfields to civilian targets in Britain. This shift saved the RAF from annihilation and gave it breathing space to repair its losses.

London now became the target for a succession of major attacks from September 7th to the end of the month. In one day, September 15th, over 1,000 German bombers and 700 fighters flew over the city, killing hundreds of civilians and reducing many of its historic buildings to ruins. British fighter pilots were on the frontline and proved brave, relentless and effective. On the 15th, they shot down 56 German planes for a loss of 26 British aircraft. After nearly a month, the fighting spirit of the RAF had done its work and the Luftwaffe refused to undertake any more daytime raids, preferring the cover of night.

The effect of these air-raids on the civilian population was profound. Parents and older people were terrified, seeing their families and homes as casualties of the brutal German assault. For children, however, a sense of fear was balanced by the novelty of the situation. Peter Newark, a schoolboy living in Romford, to the east of London, during the Battle of Britain watched the fighting at first hand in the sky above him. 'A Messerschmitt 109, a German fighter plane, flew down my

High Street in Sheffield ablaze during the night of December 12th, 1940, after a devastating bombing raid by German aircraft. As Hitler failed to defeat Britain's air defence, German bombing raids were used increasingly to terrify its population, killing tens of thousands of civilians. [Peter Newark's Military Pictures]

Soldiers delicately remove an unexploded German bomb. One in ten bombs dropped on London failed to explode and some are still uncovered today. [Peter Newark's Military Pictures]

ARP warden searches a wrecked bedroom for survivors after a German bombing raid. [Peter Newark's Military Pictures]

As RAF fighters fought with German air-craft above Britain, British bombers went after Hitler's invasion fleet, destroying a tenth of the barges and boats gathered in the ports of France and the Low Countries for Operation Sea Lion. This blow, in conjunction with the failure to break the RAF, convinced Hitler to drop his proposed invasion. The Battle of Britain had been won and a grateful Churchill made it clear that the nation's thanks should go to the pilots of the RAF, of whom he said: 'Never, in the field of human conflict, was so much owed by so many to so few.' Some 915 British airplanes had been shot down during the battle, but they had accounted for almost twice as many German aircraft. The air war against Britain, however, was far from over. Although not part of any invasion plan, intense bombing raids continued for almost a year into spring 1941 against London and other principal industrial cities. On the night of November 14th, Coventry was attacked by 500 German bombers and virtually wiped out. The air assault on Britain became known as the Blitz and over 43,000 men, women and children were killed in or near their homes, with another 50,000 badly injured. It was the worst toll ever inflicted on Britain's civilian population.

street, just above the houses and shot up the gas storage tower at the end of the road. Fortunately, it didn't explode, as it would have taken the street with it, but I rushed inside and told my Dad. 'D-d-d-d-dad,' I said, stammering badly, and he said 'stop stammering'. So, quick as a flash, I said, 'well, the King stammers', which he did [George VI] and my Dad gave me a clip round the head which I thought was a bit rich, considering what I'd just seen and what we'd just survived.' Children collected the shrapnel from bullets and shells and it was considered a good day when school was shut because of bomb damage. Little air-raid shelters were constructed in the gardens of houses for whole families to shelter in. 'I couldn't stand this,' remembered Olive Yates, a school girl at the time. 'It smelled terrible and my mother and father would always be arguing. I preferred to stay in the house and face the Luftwaffe, than go in that tiny hole with my family.'

As the principal target for Germany's terror raids, London and its people had to prepare themselves for being on the frontline. Nearly one Londoner in six became involved in some aspect of civil defence. Thousands volunteered to join the ARP (Air Raid Precautions) and AFS (Auxiliary Fire Service). ARP wardens were responsible for ensuring that everyone obeyed the new rules during air-raids, such as maintaining a complete blackout, turning off

all lights, so that bombers could not use these to identify targets. But many people regarded them as overly officious and they became a butt of many people's frustration with the new regime. Wearing white painted helmets, the most dangerous part of their job was to man the numerous look-out posts that were erected on tall buildings during bombing raids so as to pick out areas that were badly hit and on fire and send emergency services to deal with them. Sometimes the precautions caused fatalities. During the blackout, which plunged the streets of London into a depth of darkness unfamiliar to most people, up to forty people a night died through accidents. Others learned to make a business out of it, such as one lady who applied luminous paint around keyholes.

Public air-raid shelters were constructed throughout London. The great green areas of Hyde Park and Hampstead Heath were dug over with trenches reinforced with sandbags. Basements in buildings were converted for public use and brick and concrete shelters hastily built. Anderson shelters were erected in the gardens of houses for individual families, consisting of a hole in the ground covered with a piece of corrugated iron, but if it rained heavily, they frequently flooded. The women of Romford marched to their town hall, carrying placards complaining 'Sink or swim in Romford shelters' and 'Is pneumonia better than bombs?' The most

Barrage balloon rises above a British park. Groups of these balloons were used to hinder low-flying German aircraft during the Battle of Britain. [Peter Newark's Military Pictures]

popular and effective shelters were the deep shelters provided by the London Underground. As the Blitz progressed, Underground stations were provided with 200,000 bunks as well as stoves and sanitation. Even a Tube train was equipped to provide food from station to station. Most people were happy simply to lie on the platforms under a blanket.

Active air defence was provided by anti-aircraft (AA) guns and searchlights. Barrage balloons rose above London, as many as 1,000 deployed over the city, their cables being intended to hinder low-flying aircraft. These balloons frequently became the targets for enemy aircraft, but they were cheap to

American anti-aircraft artillery and searchlight unit based in Britain. After the United States entered the war against Germany in 1941, growing numbers of U.S. troops were stationed in Britain, culminating in the hundreds of thousands of soldiers that launched the D-Day invasion of France in 1944. [Peter Newark's Military Pictures]

replace and once the aircraft were drawn to them, they were often shot down by the RAF or anti-aircraft fire. Light anti-aircraft guns were placed throughout London, but the most effective guns were heavier weapons such as the 3.7 inch. Each gun weighed eight tons but could be traversed 360 degrees and fire ten shells a minute up to 41,000 feet into the air. Each gun demanded twelve crew and as men were drafted elsewhere, women took over, being the only opportunity for British women to fight directly with the enemy.

Anti-aircraft guns were organised in batteries of eight and formed a series of defensive lines from eastern to central London, flanking either side of the Thames, whose silvery reflection formed the main guide to enemy aircraft. The crew lived near the site of their gun and were only slightly protected by sandbags and corrugated iron. It was a highly dangerous job and when an air-raid started, they would fire thousands of rounds non-stop for as long as necessary, sometimes wearing out the barrel so it might explode and kill the crew. For all this, precious few

German aircraft were actually shot down by AA batteries, its purpose being admitted more one of raising morale by being seen to fire back and making it more difficult for the German pilots to carry out their murderous job. By creating fire zones, in which guns pumped thousands of shells into the air, these batteries did in fact discourage German aircraft from carrying out in full their raids or direct them elsewhere, dropping their bombs short on hapless suburbs.

The worst of the Blitz came to an end in May 1941 when Hitler decided to switch his main air resources away from trying to defeat Britain and concentrated them instead against Russia as he launched a massive invasion of that country. But this did not mean an end to air-raids on Britain and in the summer of 1944 came a new threat. Londoners noticed little aircraft whizzing through the air and then to their relief and to the pride of anti-aircraft batteries they went crashing down. 'I said to Alf,' said one Londoner, 'that the gunners were on form, three over, three down. Hardly credible. We began to discuss the possibility of them not being planes, as

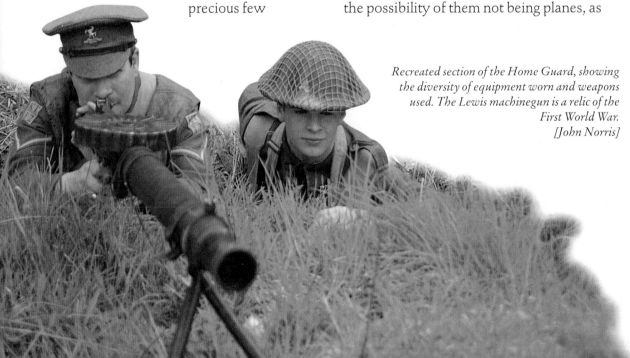

Recreated section of the Home Guard, showing the diversity of equipment worn and weapons used. The Lewis machinegun is a relic of the First World War.
[John Norris]

we could see flames coming from the tails of them, also a light in the nose.'

The little aircraft were in fact flying bombs and when each one crashed it caused great destruction. The Germans called them V-1s and they were part of Hitler's initiative to create a new generation of war-winning high technology weapons. Londoners called them buzz bombs or doodlebugs and became used to the sound they made when they flew overhead, learning to take shelter only when the engines cut out and the bomb dropped. So as to mislead the Germans to what damage they caused, there was a news blackout on the subject, but this was unpopular and led to a misleading sense of security. Over 2,000 flying bombs were launched at London and though some did very little damage, others, like a bomb that landed outside Bush House in the Aldwych, killed scores of people, largely because the bombs landed during the day when the streets and buildings were crowded. The uncertainty of where these bombs would land and the randomness of their destruction depressed civilian morale greatly, particularly as many people considered the war was coming to a close with the Allied invasion of Normandy. Worse was to come.

In September 1944, London became victim to an assault by long-range missiles, the first city ever to be so attacked. Advanced in the field of rocket engineering, German scientists had devised the V-2 missile. Too fast to be intercepted by airplanes or anti-aircraft batteries, there was no buzzing sound as they approached. All Londoners knew of an attack was the instant of destruction. The result was terrible. One missile landed in Islington and demolished 50 houses. Another landed in a

Woolworth store in Deptford and killed 168 people, 11 people simply being vaporised. A thousand men worked for 48 hours to recover the survivors. One missile landed on Smithfield market and killed 115 people.

Although the missiles were picked up on radar, there was nothing that could be done to stop them and no warning was given whatsoever. At first, it was decided not even to admit that the damage was caused by missiles, officials saying it was a gas mains explosion or such like, but the attacks became too frequent to ignore. Over a thousand missiles were launched at Britain, half of them falling on London and the majority of these on an already ravaged East End. V-1s and V-2s together destroyed over 30,000 homes and damaged 1.25 million houses in the London area alone. The suffering of the homeless was made worse by the winter of 1944-45 being the coldest for fifty years. The missile attacks only came to an end when Allied troops overran the launch sites on the Continent; finally Britain could breathe a sigh of relief after suffering five years of air assaults.

The Battle of Britain had stopped Hitler from invading the country, but it did not bring an end to Britain's readiness to face such a threat. Almost two million men served in the Home Guard, or what has affectionately become known as 'Dad's Army'. These were men outside the regular army who volunteered to fight on their own territory against any invader. This movement began as the Local Defence Volunteers, following an announcement by the Secretary of State for War, Anthony Eden, on May 14th 1940, asking for fit men between 16 and 65 years to volunteer. By the end of the month, some

Recreated unit of the 1st Airborne Reconnaissance Squadron firing a 3 inch mortar. This was an elite, information gathering unit dropped into enemy territory before the main force. They wear the camouflaged Denison smock, typical of British paratroopers at this time. [WWII Living History Association/Guy Channing]

Recreated sergeant and corporal of the Home Guard directing a military exercise. The corporal carries a non-standard .30 inch calibre U.S. designed bolt-action rifle and wears a sidecap. The sergeant is armed with a 9mm Sten sub-machinegun, wears a forage cap, and has his gasmask hanging on his chest. Both men wear leather anklets and have a 'KT' patch on their sleeves identifying them as Kent Home Guard. [John Norris]

300,000 men had come forward. Two months later, with the evacuation of the British army from Dunkirk, the need for this volunteer army became all the more urgent and Churchill insisted they be renamed the Home Guard, emphasising their vital contribution to home morale. In 1940, weapons were in short supply and, at first, the Home Guard had to make do with anything they could scavenge, from personal shotguns to home-made pikes and even weapons kept in museums. They were not full-time soldiers, still keeping their day-time occupations and training at the end of the day and over weekends. They were not paid, but because it gave an opportunity for local men to show their commitment to the war, whatever their age or circumstance, it was highly popular and battalions were frequently of double strength.

The Home Guard were mainly employed on sentry duty, guarding points of strategic importance such as factories, stations, harbours, bridges, and communications centres. During the Battle of Britain, 142,000 members of the Home Guard served with anti-aircraft units, while 7,000 were employed in coastal artillery units and a further 7,000 trained in bomb disposal. There was even a Home Guard river patrol along the Thames and 128 Americans resident in London formed the 'Red Eagles' or 1st American Squadron of the Home Guard.

As the war progressed, the Home Guard were eventually issued with battledress the same as regular soldiers as well as Lee-Enfield rifles and Bren guns. Earlier in the war there had been an attempt to provide the Home Guard with armoured vehicles, so they could defend airfields. Standard or Humber Super

Snipe car chassis were fitted with an armoured body of steel and wood. They could be armed with Bren guns or anti-tanks gun and became known as Beaverettes, after the minister for aircraft production, Lord Beaverbrook. Other, more bizarre vehicles were the result of local invention: such as the Tickler Tank in Maidenhead comprising scrap metal sheets fitted to a car with the addition of a Vickers machine gun; the Bison, a truck carrying a concrete pillbox; and the Armadillo, a lorry protected with armour made out of pebbles placed between sheets of wood.

The need for the Home Guard came to an end in December 1944, with the successful invasion of Europe, when it was officially asked to stand down, but it was not until a year later that it was finally disbanded, reluctantly so by many of its members who enjoyed its comradeship and sense of purpose. Over a thousand of its members were killed while on service and thirteen received the George Cross for bravery. Some members of the Home Guard had also functioned in a parallel and secret organisation called the Auxiliary Units. Devised by Colin Gubbins of Military Intelligence, these were a hand-picked elite of civilians who were given special training in guerrilla warfare. With many of them being country men such as gamekeepers and woodsmen, they were expected to survive behind enemy lines during any invasion, causing real havoc to the Germans. They were subject to the Official Secrets Act and were not officially enrolled as soldiers. They numbered only just over 3,500, but were trained in handling explosives and techniques of sabotage. During any invasion, they were to operate from hideouts

MINISTRY OF HEALTH *says:-*

Coughs and sneezes spread diseases

Trap the germs by using your handkerchief

Help to keep the Nation Fighting Fit

constructed underground and camouflaged on the surface. They would then emerge to place booby-traps across roads and attack enemy stores and communications centres with explosives. If captured by the enemy, because they were not officially soldiers, they would have been executed immediately.

In those dark days of 1940, Britain had never come so close to being conquered. It had a proud military history stretching back over hundreds of years in which it had grown used to victory abroad. Its last real invasion was considered to be the Norman conquest of 1066 and since then it has viewed itself as a

A Ministry of Health poster encouraging good health shows women working on an assembly line producing shells for the army. With men serving abroad as soldiers, women had to step into vital industrial jobs to keep up a supply of war material. [Peter Newark's Military Pictures]

Recreated members of the 12th Battalion, Kent Home Guard, look for enemy aircraft from a coastal site. At first, these unpaid volunteers were provided with no uniform and no weapons, having to make do with what they could salvage, including wearing World War One equipment and being armed with shotguns, but as the war progressed they were provided with a battledress and more up to date weapons. The soldier on the left wears the armband issued to all Home Guard members. [Chatham Home Guard]

Recreated members of the 1st Airborne Reconnaissance Squadron talk to a veteran of the actual regiment. They all wear the famous maroon beret. Members of the WWII Living History Association see their recreations of soldiers of this period as a living memorial to the soldiers who actually fought to defend their country. [WWII Living History Association/Guy Channing]

sovereign, independent nation which acquired a magnificent empire that stretched around the globe. In the 20th century, however, this national confidence has been shaken by two great wars. First, in the 1914-1918 war, the tremendous losses of the Western Front made it question the sagacity of intervention in foreign powerplay. Then, in 1940, Hitler's rapid conquest of western Europe and threatened invasion of Britain made it wonder whether it could even survive as an independent nation.

Such concerns have encouraged Britain to embrace international alliances in a new sense of realism. At the end of World War Two, it formalised its victorious alliance with the U.S.A. within the North Atlantic Treaty Organisation (NATO). In later years it has joining the move to European integration, although with a degree of reluctance that reflects its independent history. The story of warfare in Britain is, after all, a story of a fight for freedom from central authority, whether it be barons battling kings, or Parliament standing up to absolute monarchy.

FURTHER READING

General histories

Belloc, H., Warfare in England, London, undated.

Burne, A.H., The Battlefields of England, London, 1996.

Carver, Field Marshal Lord, Britain's Army in the 20th Century, London, 1998.

Chandler, D. (editor), History of the British Army, Oxford, 1994.

Dupuy, R.E., & Dupuy, T.N., The Encyclopedia of Military History, London, 1986.

Guest, K. & D., British Battles, London, 1996.

Henderson, D.M., The Scottish Regiments, London, 1996.

Hill, J.R. (editor), History of the Royal Navy, Oxford, 1995.

Keegan, J., The Face of Battle, London, 1976.

Makepeace-Warne, A., Companion to the British Army, London, 1995.

Newark, T., Book of Uniforms, London, 1998.

Westlake, R., English and Welsh Regiments, Staplehurst, 1995.

Recreated corporal of the 1st Airborne Reconnaissance Squadron, standing before a 1942 jeep armed with a Vickers machinegun. Every soldier in this elite unit was a volunteer. In 1944, they fought a famous last stand at Arnhem in the failed attempt to capture a bridge across the Rhine. [WWII Living History Association/ Guy Channing]

Military Illustrated, the leading military history magazine, published monthly, contains numerous articles on all aspects of warfare in Britain.

English Heritage, Register of Historic Battlefields, identifies the top battlefields of historic importance in England with details of what is being done to preserve them.

Celts and Romans

Caesar, The Conquest of Gaul, Penguin Classic, 1951.

Connolly, P., Greece and Rome at War, London, 1998.

Laing, L., Celtic Britain, London, 1979.

Newark, T., Warlords—Ancient, Celtic, Medieval, London, 1996.

Newark, T., Women Warlords, London, 1989.

Sumner, G., Roman Army: Wars of the Empire, London, 1997.

Tacitus, The Agricola and the Germania, Penguin Classic, 1948.

Webster, G., The Roman Invasion of Britain,

London, 1993.
Webster, G., Rome against Caractacus, London, 1993.

Saxons and Vikings

Anglo-Saxon Chronicle, Everyman Classic, 1972.

Griffith, P., The Viking Art of War, London, 1995.

Holmes, M., King Arthur, London, 1996.

Shadrake, D. & S., Barbarian Warriors: Saxons, Vikings, Normans, London, 1997.

Trapp, J.B., (editor), Medieval English Literature, Oxford, 1973.

Wilson, D., The Anglo-Saxons, London, 1981.

Knights and Archers

Bartlett, C., English Longbowman 1330-1515, London, 1995.

Coss, P.R., The Knight in Medieval England 1000-1400, Stroud, 1993.

Prestwich, M., Armies and Warfare in the Middle Ages—the English Experience, London, 1996.

Strickland, M., War and Chivalry, Cambridge, 1996.

Traquair, P., Freedom's Sword—Scotland's Wars of Independence, London, 1998.

Tudors and Guns

Cummins, J., Francis Drake, London, 1995.

Eltis, D., The Military Revolution in Sixteenth Century Europe, London, 1995.

Haigh, P.A., The Military Campaigns of the Wars of the Roses, Stroud, 1995.

Lander, J.R., The Wars of the Roses, Stroud, 1992.

Loades, D., The Tudor Navy, Aldershot, 1992.

Parker, G., The Military Revolution, Cambridge, 1996.

Parker, G., The Grand Strategy of Philip II, London, 1998.

Rule, M., The Mary Rose, Greenwich, 1982.

Scarisbrick, J.J., Henry VIII, London, 1968.

Royalists and Roundheads

Elliot-Wright, P.J.C., English Civil War, London, 1997.

Gentles, I., The New Model Army, Oxford, 1992.

Hainsworth, R., The Swordsmen in Power, Stroud, 1997.

Foard, G., Naseby—the Decisive Campaign, Whitstable, 1995.

Kitson, F., Prince Rupert, London, 1994.

Powell, J.R., The Navy in the English Civil War, London, 1962.

Reid, S., All the King's Armies, Staplehurst, 1998.

Roots, I., The Great Rebellion 1642-1660, Stroud, 1995.

Tincey, J., The British Army 1660-1704, London, 1994.

Georgians and Jacobites

Chandler, D., The Art of Warfare in the Age of Marlborough, Staplehurst, 1990.

Colley, L., Britons—Forging the Nation 1707-1837, London, 1992.

Duffy, C., The Military Experience in the Age of Reason, London, 1987.

Pocock, T., Battle for Empire, London, 1998.

Reid, S., King George's Army 1740-1793, three volumes, London, 1995.

Reid, S., 1745—A Military History of the Last Jacobite Rising, Staplehurst, 1996.

Rodger, N.A.M., The Wooden World: An anatomy of the Georgian Navy, London, 1986.

Redcoats and Napoleon

Brett-James, A., Life in Wellington's Army, London, 1994.

Fletcher, I., Napoleonic Wars: Wellington's Army, London, 1996.

Haythornthwaite, P.J., The Armies of Wellington, London, 1994.

Hathaway, E. (editor), A Dorset Soldier—Autobiography of Sgt. William Lawrence, Staplehurst, 1993.

Hibbert, C., Wellington, London, 1997.

Hutchinson, G., Martello Towers, Hastings, 1994.

Jones, E.H.S., The Last Invasion of Britain, Cardiff, 1950.

Kincaid, Captain J., Adventures in the Rifle Brigade, London, 1830 (reprinted 1998).

Lavery, B., Nelson's Navy, London, 1989.

Surtees, W., Twenty-Five Years in the Rifle Brigade, London, 1833 (reprinted 1996).

Victorians and Empire

Hamilton, C.I., Anglo-French Naval Rivalry 1840-1870, Oxford, 1993.

Kinross, J., Palmerston Forts of the South West, St. Austell, 1998.

Knight, I., Go to your God like a Soldier, London, 1996.

Partridge, M.S., Military Planning for the Defence of the United Kingdom, 1814-1870, Westport, 1989.

Rogers, P.G., Battle in Bossenden Wood, Oxford, 1961.

Wells, J.G., The Immortal Warrior, London, 1987.

Tommies and Poppies

Boorman, D., At the Going Down of the Sun, York, 1988.

Bull, S., World War One: British Army, London, 1998.

Fredette, R. H., The Sky on Fire—the first Battle of Britain 1917-1918, New York, 1976.

Hudson, M., & Stanier, J., War and the Media, Stroud, 1997.

Simkins, P., Kitchener's Army, Manchester, 1988.

Tucker, S.C., The Great War 1914-18, London, 1998.

Winter, J.M., The Great War and the British People, London, 1986.

Barnsley, 1998.

Marwick, A., The Home Front, London, 1976.

O'Brien, T., Civil Defence, London, 1955.

Overy, R., Why the Allies Won, London, 1995.

Schweitzer, P. (editor), What did you do in the war, Mum?, London, 1985.

Terraine, J., The Right of the Line—The Royal Air Force 1939-45, London, 1985.

Wallington, N., Firemen at War, Newton Abbot, 1981.

Weinberg, G.L., A World at Arms, Cambridge, 1994.

Westall, R., Children of the Blitz, London, 1985.

Ziegler, P., London at War 1939-1945, London, 1995.

Dad's Army and the Blitz

Beardmore, G., Civilians at War, 1984.

Calder, A., The People's War, London, 1969.

Graves, C., The Home Guard of Britain, London, 1943.

Hogg, I.V., German Secret Weapons of the Second World War, London, 1999.

Kieser, E., Hitler on the Doorstep: Operation Sea Lion, London, 1997.

McCamley, N.J., Secret Undergound Cities,

RE-ENACTMENT SOCIETIES

There are over 100 re-enactment societies throughout Britain recreating military and social life from the ancient Celts to World War Two, but the following list includes some of the best, many of them winning groups in the annual Military Illustrated Best Re-enactment Group awards.

For a list of events at which re-enactors can be seen in action around Britain, contact the Special Events Unit, English Heritage, Portland House, Stag Place, London SW1E 5EE, tel: 0171 973 3434.

Celts and Romans

Corieltauvi Tribe.
Contact: Rosemary Gibson, 83 Harrowgate Drive, Birstall, Leicester LE4 3GR.

Durotriges (Celtic).
Contact: David Freeman, New Barn field centre, Bradford Peverel, Dorset DT2 9SD, tel: 01305 267463.

Ermine Street Guard.
Contact: Chris Haines, Oakland Farm, Dog Lane, Witcombe, Gloucestershire GL3 4UG, tel: 01452 862235.

Roman Military Research Society.
Contact: Ian Post, 125 Great Meadow, Blackthorn, Northampton NN3 8DJ, tel: 01604 416050.

Legio Secunda Augusta.
Contact: David Richardson, 61 Totland Road, Portsmouth PO6 3HS, tel: 01705 369970.

Saxons and Vikings

Britannia.
Contact: Dan & Susanna Shadrake, 13
Ardleigh, Basildon, Essex SS16 5RA, tel:
01268 544511,

Milites Litoris Saxonici.
Contact: John Harris, 82 London Road,
Faversham, Kent ME13 8TA, tel: 01795
539832.

Regia Anglorum.
Contact: Kim Siddorn, 9 Durleigh close,
Headley Park, Bristol BS13 7NQ, tel: 0117
9646818.

The Vikings (N.F.P.S.).
Contact: Ben Davis, 74 Sedgwick Street,
Cambridge CB1 3AL, tel: 01223 572840.

Knights and Archers

Conquest.
Contact: John Cole, 61 King Edward's Grove,
Teddington, Middlesex TW11 9LZ, tel: 0181
977 1768.

Medieval Combat Society.
Contact: Gary Doughty, 7a Jacomb Road,
Lower Broadheath, Worcester WR2 6QW,
tel: 01905 641443.

Wolfshead Bowmen.
Contact: Heath Pye, Rosemary Cottage, 15
Tas Combe Way, Willingdon, Eastbourne
BN20 9JA, tel: 01323 503666.

Tudors and Guns

Ragged Staff Medieval Society.
Contact: Lynda Woodhouse, 35 Longfield
Road, Tring, Herts HP23 4DG, tel: 01442
824941.

White Company.
Contact: Catherine Tranter, 1 Upgate,
Poringland, Norwich, Norfolk NR14 7SH, tel:
01508 492158.

Stafford Household/Bills and Bows.
Contact: Graham Smith, 248 Wetmore Road,
Burton on Trent, Staffordshire DE14 1RB, tel:
01283 517871.

Royalists and Roundheads

Sealed Knot Society.
Contact: Ian Allen, PO Box 2000,
Nottingham, Nottinghamshire NG2 5LH, tel:
01384 295939.

English Civil War Society.
Contact: Jonathan Taylor, 70 Hailgate,
Howden, East Riding, Yorkshire DN14 7ST,
tel: 01430 430695.

Lord Robartes Regiment of Foote
Contact: Rob Butler, Plum Tree House, 46
College Street, Irthlingborough, Northants
NN9 5TX, tel: 01933 653637.

Georgians and Jacobites

White Cockade.
Contact: Michael Newcomen, 18 Mitchell Square, Blairgowie, Perthshire PH10 6HR, tel: 01250 875600.

47th Foot.
Contact: Nigel Hardacre, 60 Oakcroft, Woodend, Clayton-le-Woods, Chorley, Lancashire PR6 7UJ, tel: 01772 315192.

Histrionix.
Contact: David Edge, Bromley Cottage, Overthorpe, Banbury, Oxfordshire OX17 2AD, tel: 01295 712677.

Association of Crown Forces 1776.
Contact: Alan Haselup, Kennel House, 150 Capel Street, Capel le Ferne, Folkestone, Kent CT18 7HA.

Redcoats and Napoleon

Napoleonic Association.
Contact: Ian Barstow, 57 Station Road, Purton, Wiltshire SN5 9EL, tel: 01793 771996.

95th Rifles Regiment of Foot.
Contact: Les Handscombe, 42 Nunnery Street, Castle Hedingham, Halstead, Essex CO9 3DW, tel: 01787 461433.

12th Light Dragoons.
Contact: Martin Render, Jasmine Cottage, Fern Hill, Glemsford, Suffolk CU10 7PR, tel: 01787 280077.

Victorians and Empire

Diehard Company.
Contact: Tim Rose, 21 Addison Way, North Bersted, Bognor Regis, Sussex PO22 9HY, tel: 01243 860036.

Tommies and Poppies

Great War Society.
Contact: Geoff Carefoot, 18 Risedale Drive, Longridge, Lancashire PR3 3SB, tel: 01772 782551.

Dad's Army and the Blitz

WWII Living History Association.
Contact: David Bennett, 25 Olde Farm Drive, Darby Green, Camberley, Surrey GU17 0DU, tel: 01252 409616.

Chatham Home Guard.
Contact: Tim Schild, 43 Linwood Avenue, Strood, Rochester, Kent ME2 3TP, tel: 01634 710504.

English Heritage membership - join us today!

Over 600 special events and re-enactments such as those pictured in this book take place at our properties every year. All of them are free to our members.

But this is only one of the many benefits enjoyed by members. Others are:

- Free entry to over 400 English Heritage historic properties
- Half-price admission during the first year of membership to a further 100-plus historic properties in Scotland, Wales and the Isle of Man. In second and further years of membership, entry to these sites is free
- Annual editions of the Visitors' Handbook, a map of England showing all the properties, the Events diary and the Concerts diary
- A quarterly, full colour members' magazine, Heritage Today
- The opportunity to take part in exclusive members' events, including lectures and 'behind the scenes' visits to the properties
- The chance to take part in specially arranged members' weekend breaks and cruises
- Discounts on tickets for our summer season of concerts

But there is more. English Heritage members directly support our wide range of conservation work.

- We are the government's official advisor on listed buildings, scheduled monuments, and conservation areas.
- We highlight worrying issues like the numbers of historic buildings that are at risk from neglect.

- We give millions of pounds in grants each year to archaeological projects, cathedrals and churches, decaying inner cities, and historic houses.
- We have an internationally acclaimed Education Service which provides information and resources for teachers and educational organisations from primary level right through to tertiary level and GNVQs.
- We publish scores of guidance notes and guidance on conservation issues.

We look to the future too because we believe that the heritage is not just about the past. Today's architecture is tomorrow's historic building, and so we support innovative modern architecture and design, and advise on protection through listing for our major modern buildings.

All these activities and more are supported by government grant, but also directly by the income we receive from our members and visitors. So your contribution goes directly towards preserving England's wonderful past and exciting present for future generations to enjoy.

To become a member or to find out more:

- phone our Customer Services Department on 01793 414910; or
- write to us at English Heritage, Freepost, WD214, PO Box 570, Swindon SN2 2UR; or
- e-mail us at members@english-heritage.org.uk; or
- consult our website at http://www.english-heritage.org.uk

INDEX